THE DEATHS OF THE AUTHOR

Jane Gallop

::

THE DEATHS OF THE AUTHOR

::

Reading

and

Writing

in Time

Duke University Press :: *Durham & London* :: 2011

© 2011 Duke University Press

All rights reserved.

Printed in the United States

of America on acid-free paper ∞

Designed by Amy Ruth Buchanan

Typeset in Bembo by Tseng

Information Systems, Inc.

Library of Congress Cataloging-

in-Publication Data appear on the

last printed page of this book.

::

CONTENTS

::

vii   Acknowledgments

1   Introduction

27   PART I. *The Friendly Return of the Author*

29   1. The Author Is Dead but I Desire the Author

55   2. The Ethics of Indecency

85   PART II. *If I Were a Writer and Dead*

87   3. The Queer Temporality of Writing

115   4. The Persistent and Vanishing Present

145   Notes

163   Works Cited

167   Index

::

ACKNOWLEDGMENTS

::

Over the six years I worked on this book, I know I benefited from comments and efforts of more people than I can here thank, indeed more than I can remember. There are, however, a few people whose help I want in particular to acknowledge.

Ken Wissoker continues to be for me the best possible editor in how he combines encouragement with demand in a way that forces me to work harder and be less self-indulgent. His warm but professional interventions have encouraged me to try harder at revision than I ever had before, than I had thought possible. However successful I have been in putting this book together, without Ken this book would not have been even half as coherent.

Two friends pointed me in directions which were crucial for the ultimate shape of this book. Nancy K. Miller suggested I read Derrida's collection of mourning essays; Ellen McCallum invited me to contribute to a volume on queer temporality. These two conversations led directly to chapters 2 and 3 of the present book.

While Ellen first directed me toward queer temporality, my companion in exploring that territory has been Kate Haffey. Kate was beginning to work toward her dissertation in queer temporality at the moment she became my research assistant, the moment I started work on chapter 3. Kate remained my assistant for three years, reading and discussing drafts as this book took shape. She defended her marvelous dissertation and received her doctorate as I was finishing this book. Her last task as my assistant was sending this manuscript off to the press. Having Kate's assistance has been invaluable to this book: not only is she always an attentive reader and herself a wonderful writer, but her involvement in queer temporality and my learning from her dissertation has definitely influenced the shape this book has taken.

::

::

Several years ago, I found myself reading a book just a few months after the author had died.[1] The recent death lent a poignancy to my reading, and I thought to myself, "This book is haunted by the death of the author." And so it was that, in response to this particular reading experience, a set phrase from literary theory — "the death of the author" — popped into my head. It is a familiar slogan, efficiently and evocatively representing the poststructuralist dismissal of the author, signifying polemically that the author does not matter, only the text — that we should not care about the author. Yet in my recent experience what had become a theoretical cliché suddenly took on, as it were, new life. While "the death of the author," as poststructuralist catchphrase, signified a way to rid the text of the author, I found that the author's death could make the reader think more not less about the author. The present book arose out of that defamiliarization of the theoretical commonplace.

I am far from the first to have had occasion to hear new meanings in the overly familiar phrase. It could happen any time someone schooled in literary theory is faced with an author's death. For example, in a 1989 article, responding to the *fatwa* calling precisely for the author Salman Rushdie's death, Gayatri Chakravorty Spivak cites the poststructuralist death of the author and wonders how we are to read it in this situation. Mentioning that the phrase has "become a slogan," Spivak tries to reopen its meaning.[2] While Spivak's cogent rethinking of the death of the author lasts only a page before she goes on to her reading of Rushdie's *Satanic Verses*, the present book will dedicate itself to this opening up of the poststructuralist slogan. The project of this book is to bring into literary theory other seemingly more anecdotal meanings of the phrase.

:: :: ::

In the 1980s, the phrase was widely used in the American literary academy, referring to a general current coming from France, from poststructuralism, from newly theoretical literary studies. The death of the author was controversial — under attack both by older-style humanist critics and by newer political assaults on the exclusivity of the canon. The slogan was taken to represent a wide swath of French literary theory. Researching the phrase's usage, I discovered that critics who use it generally refer the reader to two articles — and by and large to only two articles — always the same two, which appeared within a year of each other, one by Roland Barthes in 1968 and the other by Michel Foucault in 1969. Barthes and Foucault were such big names in our star-based reception of poststructuralism, and different enough from each other, that this confluence of two articles was able by itself to represent an entire theoretical trend.

In February 1969, Michel Foucault presented a paper in Paris entitled "What is an Author?" that historicizes the concept of the author by examining the diverse ways the concept has functioned in different historical moments.[3] Although this paper is almost always cited as a source for the death of the author, it actually relegates that topic to one and only one of its more than three dozen paragraphs. While Foucault's paper is in fact only concerned in a very minor way with the death of the author, because it has been taken for decades as one of the two sources of the infamous phrase, I want to look briefly at what Foucault says in that single paragraph. I will also touch on the lecture's immediate reception, where we can see that single paragraph overshadowing the rest of the paper.

Early in his lecture, Foucault devotes a paragraph to what he calls the "familiar theme" of "the kinship between writing and death" (793, 116). This kinship "inverts an age-old theme"—Foucault represents the ancient theme with brief mentions of how Greek epics were "destined to perpetuate the hero's immortality" and how, in *A Thousand and One Nights*, the story had "for motivation, for theme and pretext, to not die." Having thus sketched this age-old relation, he dramatically states the reversal: "This theme of . . . writing made to ward off death, our culture has metamorphosed it; writing is now tied to sacrifice, to the sacrifice of life itself. . . . The work whose duty it was to bring immortality has now received the right to kill, to be the murderer of its author" (793, 117).

For centuries writing was thought to bring immortality; now it brings death. In his account of this turn, Foucault repeats the word "now" (*maintenant*)—"writing is *now* tied to sacrifice," "the work has *now* received the right to kill" (emphasis added). And yet, despite this emphasis on the nowness of the turn, Foucault is not announcing something new but instead treats it as something already well established, a "familiar theme." The paragraph concludes with this sentence: "All this is known; and for quite some time criticism and philosophy have taken note of this disappearance or this death of the author."[4]

Foucault ends his brief discussion of writing's relation to death on the phrase "death of the author." "The Death of the Author" is in fact the title of the essay by Roland Barthes published just the year before Foucault's lecture. Foucault does not mention Barthes's essay.

"The Death of the Author" is a short polemical piece, a manifesto published in a small literary quarterly. "What is an Author?"—presented to an august assemblage of philosophers, scholars, and intellectuals[5] — is a nuanced consideration of the various ways in which the author has functioned in different historical moments. Foucault's exploration of the author, while more than three times as long as Barthes's manifesto, has nonetheless generally been overshadowed by the latter.

The French publication of "What is an Author?" includes not just Foucault's paper but also the discussion that followed the lecture. The bulk of the discussion is a long question by Lucien Goldmann and Foucault's answer to that question. Goldmann focuses on the death of the author, despite its being a rather minor point of the lecture, and does indeed find it familiar, part of the larger current of structuralism, "which notably includes the names of Lévi-Strauss, Roland Barthes, Althusser, Derrida, etc."[6] Goldmann is thus the first to inscribe "What is an Author?" as part of a larger critical current.

The transcription of the session shows Foucault clearly frustrated by this response to his lecture. In his reply to Goldmann, Foucault insists that the theme of the author's death is not his. From the moment of its delivery, and throughout the following decades, "What is an Author?" has all too often been received as seconding "The Death of the Author." As Spivak puts it in 1989, "Foucault's question 'What is an Author?' has been construed by most readers as a rhetorical question to be answered in the negative."[7] I see this misprision of "What is an Author?" as part of the slogan-effect of "the death of the author."

Wanting to go back and reconsider the death of the author, to get beyond the theoretical slogan, my research consistently suggested I look at two short French texts from the late sixties. Reading those two articles, I discover that it is really not even two but to a single text we should turn. The present book will thus begin by going back to Roland Barthes's "The Death of the Author."

My first chapter returns to Barthes, to see what he meant by the catchphrase and also to get a fuller sense of his theory of the author. I read the notorious 1968 essay along with a broader corpus of his writings on the topic. In Barthes's writing about authors, I find actually two deaths — the abstract, polemical death of the slogan and a moving, more bodily death of the mortal author. The attempt to connect the two deaths, to think the abstract theoretical death along with the real loss of the author, is the project of the present book. The title of this book, *The Deaths of the Author*, is meant to refer to both the literary theoretical concept and the real life drama, to make it impossible to think either separately, to insist we think them together.

The first chapter discovers that, far from a simple dismissal, for Barthes the death of the author actually institutes a relation in which the reader desires the author. The title of chapter 1, "The Author Is Dead but I Desire the Author," is a statement I found in Barthes's 1974 book *The Pleasure of the Text*. I think this statement gives us a fuller picture of Barthes's theorization of the author. This striking statement professes his perverse desire for the author he nonetheless knows to be dead. I call the desire in this assertion "perverse" to connect it to the celebration of non-normative sexuality that is central to *The Pleasure of the Text*. In this declaration of desire, however, what is literally perverse is carried by the conjunction "but," by the stubborn unreasonableness of desiring despite the knowledge that someone is dead. Focusing on Barthes's relation to the author not only provides a more nuanced, less abstract understanding of the death of the author, it also allows us to read the high literary theorist as at the same time a perverse, even queer, desiring subject. The present book is a reconsideration of the death of the author in the era of queer theory.

In 1992, Seán Burke published *The Death and Return of the Author*, drawing attention to the fact that not only did Barthes declare the author dead in 1968, but three years later, in his book *Sade, Fourier, Loyola*, he announced the author's return. I share Burke's sense that Barthes's theory of the author includes the return of the author pronounced dead, but unlike Burke I am interested in the adjective that accompanies Barthes's announcement in 1971 of the return: "The pleasure of the Text also includes a friendly return of the author."[8] Part I of the present book gets its title from this sentence, directing us to focus on the odd and intriguing notion of a "friendly return."

While Burke's book—keeping the theoretical concept of the author separate from any personal, anecdotal, or erotic meanings—ultimately moves in a different direction than our current project, I remain particularly grateful to Burke for prompting me to reread *Sade, Fourier, Loyola*, which I had not looked at since working on Sade in the seventies. The preface to it contains Barthes's longest theoretical consideration of the author outside the essay from 1968. My first chapter is centered on the 1971 preface, and includes a slow, detailed reading of the paragraph from this preface that opens by announcing the "friendly return of the author." This dense, rich paragraph offers us in fact not only the title for part I, but also—in its last sentence—a phrase to entitle part II. Not only is this beautiful, crazy paragraph the heart of the first chapter, it is also at the theoretical core of the book.

While the first chapter spends some time wondering about the word "friendly" in this paragraph, about what sort of relation it connotes, and how it connects to perverse desire, the idea of the friend takes center stage in my second chapter. Where Barthes's "friendly" is part of a theorization of the author, in chapter 2 we find Jacques Derrida reading texts authored by personal friends who have just died. The second chapter considers Derrida's memorial essays for his friends (collected in the 2001 volume *The Work of Mourning*), focusing in particular on how Derrida reads his friends' texts as part of his mourning.

Part I of the present book—"The Friendly Return of the Author"—is composed of these two chapters. The first returns to the theoretician of "The Death of the Author" in order to open up the theory to a more nuanced, affective understanding of the reader's relation to the author. Yet even with its addition of poignancy, mortality, and desire, the first chapter remains on the level of theory; the author's death remains a theoretical death. The second chapter, on the other hand, considers a much more personal relation to the author's death, a reader's mourning for a dear, departed author.

While chapter 1 articulates an erotic relation to the dead author, chapter 2 is concerned with an ethical relation to the other whose words we are reading. Despite this difference in registers, both end up taking a stance in perversity, in the sort of logical perversity represented by conjunctions like "but" or "and yet." Barthes knows the author is dead *but* nonetheless desires him; Derrida feels that these memorials to his dead friends are "indecent" *and yet* he writes and publishes them just the same. I title the second chapter "The Ethics of Indecency" to capture Derrida's earnest perversity.

In the first memorial essay Derrida ever wrote, he says: "What I believed impossible, indecent, unjustifiable . . . was to write . . . 'in memory of' those who when alive would have been my friends, present enough to me that . . . some analysis or 'study' would seem to me in that moment strictly intolerable."[9] What Derrida found intolerable, indecent, were writings that combined mourning and work. And yet that is just what he is doing, for the first time, in this 1981 text on his friend Roland Barthes who had died the previous year. Derrida declares the indecency of what he is doing in the very essay where he is doing it.

Derrida found it "impossible, indecent, unjustifiable" upon the death of his friends to write about his friends' texts as he does other texts, to treat his recently departed friends as he does other authors—that is, to treat them as authors. Yet that in fact is what he does, for the first time in 1981, but then at least 15 more times in the next two decades. This contradictory stance is what I am calling the ethics of indecency.

In the 1981 memorial to Barthes, Derrida lays out three possible relations a reader can have to the author: (1) "authors dead long before I read them," (2) "authors living at the moment we read them," and (3) "upon the death and after the death of those we have also 'known,' met, loved, etc." (76–77). Derrida finds the first two relations relatively easy; the third is the one he finds intolerable—the relation where someone passes, moves from the category of the living to the dead. What is really troubling is neither the living nor the dead author but precisely what we might call the death of the author.

While Derrida never mentions Barthes's essay "The Death of

the Author" in this piece, I nonetheless find in Derrida's memorial for Barthes a contribution to the theorization of the author's death. This essay written in response to the death of his friend combines the personal sense of loss with a more general theory of the author. This very combination goes to the heart of the theoretical ambition of the present book—a reconceptualization of the death of the author so as to include inextricably both theory and personal loss.

Derrida entitles his 1981 memorial "The Deaths of Roland Barthes." In homage to Derrida's title, I am calling this book *The Deaths of the Author.* I want to suggest how Derrida's memorial essay can be read as expanding on, twisting, and pluralizing Barthes's infamous little 1968 essay.[10]

In the tri-partite classification of possible relations to the author found in Derrida's memorial for Barthes, the confrontation with the death of the author includes a relation to that person, someone we have "met," if not "loved." While the typology would aim to be generalizable, putting all authors in categories, the third category, unlike the first two, includes not only the author's existential status, but the reader's personal connection to the author. We have here an example of theorization that is not abstracted from personal connection.

And not abstracted from temporality. Here is how Derrida introduces his typology: "There are, in the *time* that relates us to texts and their signatories . . . three possibilities" (76). Derrida italicizes the word "time." This is a theorization of the author with an insistence on the moment of reading: "long dead before I read them," "living *at the moment* we read them." In Derrida's attempt to figure out why the memorial essay is so troubling, he rethinks the reader's relation to the author in a way that focuses on that relation's temporality.

Derrida theorizes the relation to the author as part and parcel of his thinking about the genre in which he is writing. Immediately after presenting his typology of three possible relations to the author, he applies the categories to his own experience, not just his experience as a reader but rather his experience as a writer:

"Thus: I have had occasion to write about . . . texts whose authors were dead long before I read them or whose authors are living at the moment I write. . . . But what I believed impossible, indecent, unjustifiable . . . was to write *upon the death* . . . of those who when alive would have been my friends" (77). Derrida insists here not only on the moment of reading but also on the moment of writing. In Derrida's memorial for Barthes, I find a rethinking of the death of the author that it inextricable from the fact of reading in time and likewise from writing in time. This rethinking is central to the present book, and is represented by the book's subtitle, *Reading and Writing in Time*.

Appearing thus in Derrida's memorial to Barthes, which is the center of our second chapter, the question of time becomes much more prominent in chapters 3 and 4, the last two chapters of the present book. The importance of temporality is reflected in the titles of these two chapters: I call the last chapter "The Persistent and Vanishing Present"; chapter 3 is titled "The Queer Temporality of Writing." Both of these last two chapters were written under the influence of a notion called "queer temporality." That phrase, first used in a 2002 essay by Stephen Barber and David Clark, has since come to name a powerful current within the larger stream of queer theory. If the present book is a reconsideration of the death of the author in the era of queer theory, chapters 3 and 4 rethink the author's death more precisely in the era of queer temporality.

As I move from the first pair to the second pair of chapters, from part I to part II of this book, I also move from a focus on reading to a focus on writing. While Derrida does touch on writing as well as reading in his "Deaths of Roland Barthes," the first two chapters largely consider the author's death from the reader's perspective. In contrast, my last two chapters tend to look at the death of the author from the writer's point of view.

To get a title for this book's second half, I return to the same paragraph from *Sade, Fourier, Loyola* that supplied the title to part I. This paragraph in which Barthes announces the author's return is largely written from the point of view of the reader: for example, "The author . . . comes from his text and goes into our life." But in the last sentence of that paragraph, we find Barthes suddenly imagining himself in the position of the writer: "If I were a writer, and dead, how I would love it if my life . . . could . . . come to touch . . . some future body. . . ."[11] Barthes's strange fantasy here—"if I were a writer, and dead"—provides a title for part II.

As Barthes thinks the return of the dead author, he shifts, within the same paragraph, from the perspective of the reader to that of the writer. As if to really move beyond the flat and lifeless polemic against the author, Barthes must ultimately pass from the reader's standpoint to speaking as a writer. The present book follows Barthes in this move. The final two chapters reflect on how the death of the author looks to the writer writing.

Chapter 3 continues my inquiry into the memorial essay, turning to two memorials written by Eve Kosofsky Sedgwick. Sedgwick's essays belong very much to the same genre as those I consider in chapter 2: they combine personal mourning with intellectual work. Thus the third chapter continues the exploration of personal meanings for the death of the author, but whereas Derrida mourns as a reader, Sedgwick's memorials focus much more on her feelings as a writer.

As her 1990 "Memorial for Craig Owens" opens, we are not only in the same configuration we saw in Derrida's memorials, mourning the death of the author/friend, but also in the relation theorized by Barthes, where the author comes from his text and enters the reader's life. Thus, at the beginning of Sedgwick's first memorial, we find ourselves in the territory traversed in the first two chapters, in part I of the present book. Owens enters Sedgwick's life as an author, and that is his position at the beginning of her memorial, but by the end of this memorial, as she focuses on her own writing, Owens becomes more reader than author. By the end of her first memorial, Sedgwick is mourning not so much the loss of a beloved author, but something we might call the death of the reader.

"Memorial for Craig Owens" talks about an article Sedgwick is in the middle of writing, an article inspired by Owens's work, an article she was hoping Owens would read. Speaking at a memorial service for Owens, Sedgwick in fact talks at some length about what a hard time she has been having writing her article. While I find such focus on her writing difficulties in this context a bit shocking—perhaps indecent—I also find it theoretically rich. Viewed from within the drama of writing, death takes on some particular resonances. While death is generally a reminder of the fragility of life, the story Sedgwick tells about her reaction to Owens's death is about the fragility of writing, a fragility that has everything to do with writing's temporal aspect. Thinking through death from within her writing practice, Sedgwick brings to light the haunted temporality of writing.

Both of Sedgwick's memorial pieces were published in her 1993 book, *Tendencies*, the book that is her most self-conscious contribution to queer theory—her only book to foreground the idea of queer—and the central place of her two mourning essays in this book helps us read them as part of that theory. Both essays are in honor of a gay man who died of AIDS, and the incorporation of these memorials in her work bespeaks the way that mourning became a central part of queer theory. While for Derrida the connection between mourning and theoretical insight seemed unjustifiable and indecent, for Sedgwick, writing in the context of queer ethics in response to AIDS, this connection looks quite different. Queer theory in the early nineties was energized and politically justified by the embrace of precisely such indecencies.

Sedgwick's memorials include both the explicitly perverse desire for the dead we found in Barthes's writing with the mourning and grieving we read in Derrida's essays. In the texts we read in the first two chapters, Barthes could desire the dead but only abstractly and thus without grief; Derrida, on the other hand, could grieve his loss but only while feeling abashed by his own indecency. The context of queer theory in the early 1990s—trying to affirm perverse, stigmatized desire in the face of AIDS and death—made it not only possible but crucial to articulate at one and the same time both desire and loss, both radical perversity and grief. The theoretical advance produced in the present book (in part I), by bringing Derrida's mourning pieces into conjunction with Barthes's desire for the dead author, is, I would say, already operative in Sedgwick's queer memorials.

Our reading of Sedgwick in chapter 3 is guided by Stephen Barber's and David Clark's 2002 essay "Queer Moments: The Performative Temporalities of Eve Kosofsky Sedgwick." Positing the notion of Sedgwick's "queer temporality," that essay uses for the first time a phrase that has since come to name a major trend within queer theory. Where Barber and Clark derive Sedgwick's queer temporality from the foreword to *Tendencies*, I look at how this temporality plays out in and around her memorial writing in the same volume.

While the temporality of Sedgwick's first memorial is already haunted, it is in her second memorial, written a year later, that the temporality becomes particularly queer, downright indecent. The second memorial piece, originally delivered at an academic conference, is, according to Sedgwick, an "obituary" for Michael Lynch. This so-called obituary, however, was read at the conference in May 1991 while Lynch was still alive.

As she is writing the memorial for Lynch in early 1991, not only is Sedgwick facing her friend's imminent death, she is also grappling with the news that she herself has advanced, metastasized cancer. "Now, shock and mourning gaze in both directions through the obituary frame," she says in the Lynch memorial.[12] While the "obituary frame" is the genre of writing she is undertaking, the "frame" here is quite explicitly something that can be "gazed through." Sedgwick calls her memorial for Lynch "White Glasses" after the white-framed glasses that both she and Lynch wore at the time, glasses she bought in imitation of his. The gaze here goes "in both directions," as if Sedgwick and Lynch were sharing a single pair, looking at each other through the same glasses. And what their mutual gaze shares is the obituary frame; both gaze with shock and mourning at someone who is dying. Seeing through Lynch's eyes, writing with his glasses on, Sedgwick in "White Glasses" prospectively mourns her own death.

Since Lynch is still alive, the mourning for him is likewise prospective, premature. Although Sedgwick will go on to live many years after Lynch dies, in this particular moment in early 1991, both find themselves in what Sedgwick will later talk about as a transitional time "that extends from diagnosis until death."[13] "White Glasses" places the obituary writer and her subject together in a queer moment where the dead are not yet dead and the living no longer quite living. In Sedgwick's uncanny memorial, not only is the subject of the obituary disturbingly not yet dead, but the obituary is haunted by its writer's death.

In the Owens memorial, Sedgwick is looking at death from within the writing experience, but it is the reader's death mourned there. A year later, Sedgwick is once again facing death while writing, but this time she can see herself as a dying writer. This time she writes under the threat of the author's death.

By the time "White Glasses" is published (first in 1992, and then again in *Tendencies* in 1993), Lynch has died. Although a line is appended to the end of the essay giving the date of his death, the "obituary" is otherwise not revised. We can still read its peculiar (indecent) temporality as an obituary for someone still alive. "The Queer Temporality of Writing" (our third chapter) ends by connecting this refusal to revise (and thus normalize the memorial's temporality) with a statement Sedgwick makes in an interview conducted in 2000: "That's the wonderful thing about the printed word—it can't be updated instantly. It's allowed to remain anachronistic."[14]

Sedgwick chooses to "allow" her memorial for Lynch to "remain anachronistic" even before it is printed, when she could update if she chose. Instead of being, as most of us are, embarrassed by the queer temporality of the printed word, Sedgwick would embrace and celebrate it.[15] While a writer can revise and update if she chooses, the printed word is the province not of the writer but of the author. The printed word, necessarily anachronistic, is where the writer confronts her status as a dead author.

This confrontation, first glimpsed as we close our third chapter, is precisely the drama we follow in chapter 4, by looking at the temporality of writing in and around Gayatri Chakravorty Spivak's 1999 book *A Critique of Postcolonial Reason*. Spivak's response to the anachronism of the printed word would seem to be the very opposite of Sedgwick's. Where Sedgwick applauds the moment when we are "allowed" to remain anachronistic, when we cannot update, Spivak devotes more than a dozen years to updating her manuscript, and adds a large number of long footnotes endlessly trying to bring the book up to date before it becomes "printed word." Guided by a sense that the printed word's anachronism connotes the writer's confrontation with the death of the author, we focus in our last chapter on Spivak's persistent, even desperate, attempt to bring her book up to date.

The subtitle to Spivak's 1999 book is *Toward a History of the Vanishing Present*; the book's preface tells us that "the text seeks to catch the vanishing present."[16] Our chapter reads the subtitle's evocative "vanishing present" within the relation suggested by this statement in the preface. The "text"—by which she means the book she is prefacing—is trying to, wants to, "catch" the present. The present is the book's object of desire: elusive, fleeting—i.e., vanishing. The book is motivated by this pursuit of the present, but there is a sense of extreme difficulty—futility even—in seeking to catch something "vanishing."

In a footnote to her last chapter, Spivak says, "We cannot keep up with the vanishing present." This admission of futility appears in a note that is in fact trying to "keep up," trying to bring things up to date. Appended to a discussion of the Japanese firm *Comme des Garçons*, a discussion based on a 1984 article and written in the mid-1980s, the complete footnote reads: "These are the laws that, as the morning news in New York City reports on 12 Mar. 1998, are making Japanese entrepreneurs hang themselves. We cannot keep up with the vanishing present. Readers will remember that time as the era when finance capital came crashing down in the Asia-Pacific."[17]

This footnote dates a present (March 12, 1998), which is contrasted not only with a past (the text talks about things as they were "in 1984"), but also with a future (a moment that will see

March 1998 as a past "era"). This note is an encounter with the temporality of books, the temporality of authorship. The past is the moment of writing (years before publication); the future is the anticipated moment of reading; the present is when the author adds a note to try and update the text at the last moment before publication. More than a dozen years after drafting the text, Spivak makes a final attempt to bring things up to date, yet she is at the very same time acutely aware that, once published, the text will become out of date for future readers. As the author imagines her future readers, she imagines our present, one that relegates her to the past. I read this as a version of the writer's encounter with the death of the author.

Our fourth chapter thus, like our third, looks at the death of the author from the writer's perspective. Where chapter 3 looked at the occasional moment of writing in confrontation with literal death, chapter 4 considers the more general theoretical dilemma of obsolescence. Where Sedgwick writes in the shadow of death, facing not only the loss of friends but her own diagnosis with a life-threatening illness, it is not death that forces Spivak to imagine herself as a dead author; rather it is her attempt finally to write a book.

In a 1986 interview, Spivak talks about the manuscript she is then working on; this manuscript will be published thirteen years later as *A Critique of Postcolonial Reason*. In this interview she speaks about the manuscript as if it is her first book. "I'm not a book writer . . . nevertheless I think the time has come to take the plunge," she says.[18] Up until this moment, she has been "an essayist rather than a book writer": we might understand this difference between "essayist" and "book writer" as the difference between writer and author. For Spivak, "the time has come" for her to be an author.

In Spivak's magnum opus we can read the marks of her encounter with the temporality of bookwriting, with the temporality of authorship. I appreciate these marks as a contribution to theorizing authorship, as a prolonged and moving reflection on the dilemma of a writer all too aware of the necessary anachronism of the printed word, struggling with the fact that to be an author is inevitably to be a dead author, past not present. While it is our reading of Sedgwick in chapter 3 that leads us to understand Spivak's persistent revision as a writer's struggle with the death of the author, Spivak also addresses the literary theoretical concept directly in her 1999 book. As our reference earlier in this introduction to her 1989 essay on Rushdie's *Satanic Verses* suggests, the death of the author is an idea she is thinking about during the period she is working on (revising) this book.

In *A Critique of Postcolonial Reason*, Spivak cites Barthes's infamous phrase in order to situate her own reading practice. She says the reading she practices, while including the kind of "deicide/parricide" represented by Barthes's phrasing, always combines and offsets that author-murder with "complicity." In order to explain the mixture of violence and complicity that constitutes the relation to the author in her practice of reading she writes, "Even if we question the authority of Marx, his ghost keeps (us) going" (98).

Marx's ghost is Spivak's elaboration on, revision of, the death of the author. Spivak's take on the author's death does not deny that the author is dead, but it refuses that death any finality: the author is dead but his ghost keeps (us) going. Spivak's ghost takes us back to where we were at the end of our first chapter, with a sense of the author as dead but still with us, with the reader. Speaking as a reader, Spivak finds the author's ghost enabling: he keeps us going. That ghost is, however, a more disturbing figure for her as a writer, for her as an author. Here is how Spivak opens the Marx section of her book: "Marx keeps moving for a Marxist as the world moves. I keep wanting to write this section differently. . . . But . . . it is too late to undertake so radical a rewriting" (67–70). I read the Marx who "keeps moving" as the same figure as the ghost who "keeps going" thirty pages later. While it is only when she speaks as a reader that Spivak explicitly treats Marx as a dead-but-still-going author, it is here where she speaks as a writer, here where she speaks as the book's author, that Marx's ghostlike uncanny persistence is connected to her frustration at not being able to bring her book up to date. It is precisely this connection between the dead author and the impossible quest for an up-to-date book that is the subject of our fourth and final chapter.

The figure of the ghost revitalizes Marx, making him while still dead also in some way alive, so the long-dead writer can keep going. Spivak, on the other hand, while still literally alive cannot keep moving; she is stuck in the past, cannot bring the book into the present. The ghost resonates, ironically, with the fact that, while still alive, as an author Spivak is thus also already "dead."

While Marx's ghost is a figure used to make a general point about authors, it is probably not coincidental that Spivak talks about the death of the author in the section of her book on Marx. Marx is not just one of the authors Spivak reads; he is a model for her as a writer. In the very last sentence of her book, Spivak compares what she is trying to do in her writing to what Marx did. As she brings her book to a close, thus putting her writing definitively in the past, she compares herself to the writer who exemplifies for her the dead author, the author as ghost.

In my third chapter, I point out how in the foreword to *Tendencies* Sedgwick puts herself in the place of Audre Lorde, a poet who had just died of cancer. Sedgwick, as I put it there, is identifying with the dead author. At the end of *A Critique of Postcolonial Reason*, Spivak is doing the same thing, identifying with Marx, with the specific figure she has cast as the dead author. While Sedgwick identifies with a writer who died just the year before Sedgwick authors her book, Spivak identifies with an author whose literal death occurred long before she was born. What is at stake in Spivak's relation to the dead author is not literal death, but something we might call theoretical death, the threat that Marx's work will be relegated to the past, deemed no longer relevant. Taking Marx as her model at the moment the world proclaims the death of Marxism, Spivak writes in fear of becoming not a literally dead author, but something possibly even worse, an author who, while still alive, is already a ghost — outmoded, obsolete, not present but stuck in the past.

It is this relation to the author's theoretical death that in my last chapter brings us back to Barthes, back to where the present book begins. My first chapter, following Barthes, reconsiders the theoretical death of the author from the point of view of the reader. While a closer look at Barthes makes us see that the reader still has feelings for the dead author, the death in that chapter remains theoretical. It is in the second chapter, as we move to Derrida's mourning essays, that we begin to think about literal, personal death as part of our understanding of the death of the author. Reading Barthes and Derrida together, we move to a conception of the author's death that includes both the theoretical and the personal. After the analysis in these first two chapters, the death of the author has become much more nuanced, meaningful, and fraught, but it is still being approached solely from the reader's perspective.

Sedgwick's memorial writing shares with Derrida's a concern with actual, personal death, but in her case the point of view is not so much the reader's but the writer's. Our reading of Sedgwick gives us a glimpse at how the author's death shadows the writer writing, leaving its mark in the writer's engagement with temporality. Following the track of that temporal engagement, we come to read Spivak's drama of revising her book, finding in it yet another sort of encounter with the death of the author—this one like Sedgwick's from the writer's point of view, but like Barthes's concerned with theoretical rather than personal death. Taken together, our four chapters aim to revitalize the overly familiar death of the author so that we take it as both-theoretical-and-personal—so that we can take a fuller measure of its moving and unsettling effects on readers and writers, on reading and writing.

:: :: ::

Jacques Derrida died in October 2004; a few months later the journal *differences* asked if I would write for a memorial issue, and I accepted. Derrida was an author whose work had been enormously influential for me—someone I had long read and frequently taught, someone I had written about, and (to recall the categories from his memorial for Barthes) someone I had in fact met on several occasions, someone I had seen live.

By late 2004 I had begun working on this book although, as so often happens, the project as then conceived differed considerably from what it has become. Not yet actually writing chapters, I did have in mind a title, "The Ethics of Close Reading." As background to such a project, I was reading my way through the field of "ethical criticism," a reading list that drew my attention in particular to the work of Emmanuel Lévinas. When *differences* asked me to write about Derrida's work and my work, I decided to write about the only book by Derrida sitting on my desk at the time, his *Adieu à Emmanuel Lévinas.*

This 1997 volume is made up of two texts: "Adieu," a short piece Derrida delivered at Lévinas's funeral in late 1995, and the much longer "Le mot d'accueil" (translated as "A Word of Welcome"), the opening address at a conference on Lévinas's work a year later. While "Le mot d'accueil" is a greeting, "Adieu" would seem to be the very opposite, a farewell. That this book contains a welcome along with an adieu—that it contains a welcome within an adieu—suggests that these are not just opposites. If we connect the two titles respectively to hospitality and death (the two themes of the book, I would say), we might see this double title pointing to a relation between hospitality and death—that the book is looking for an ethics of hospitality toward the dead. If I were still writing a book on the ethics of close reading, I would want to connect it to this ethics of hospitality toward the dead. I would certainly want to connect this hospitality toward the dead with Barthes's notion (considered in the first chapter here) that even though the author is dead there are nonetheless authors we "live with," authors we welcome into the texture of our life.[19]

Although in 2004 I accepted the journal's invitation to write a memorial for Derrida, I nonetheless tried not to digress too far from my project on the ethics of close reading. I had bought *Adieu à Emmanuel Lévinas* as a secondary text, thinking only of my need to understand Lévinas, but in the months between purchase and reading the author had died, and I found myself reading the book with another set of questions. While working on Derrida's book on Lévinas, I became aware that he had actually written quite a number of such memorials, and I began to feel an obligation to study the whole body of his memorial essays, and to write on them sooner rather than later. And so it was that, in the year after Derrida's death, I came to write a chapter about his mourning essays. The topic of the chapter was, unbeknownst to me at the time, a large step toward a new book topic, an irreversible step toward a book, not on the ethics of close reading, but on the death of the author.

My short memorial essay for Derrida is at best a preliminary to the more comprehensive, concerted study of Derrida's mourning essays that became chapter 2 of this book. Looking back at it as I put together *The Deaths of the Author*, however, there is one thing I would want to retain from the memorial for Derrida, one thing that is not in the later, more substantial, text. In the 2005 essay, I can see something that gets at the purpose and even the ethics of the present book. I thus include here (in italics) a couple of pages from "Reading Derrida's Adieu":[20]

:: :: ::

Speaking at Lévinas's funeral, Derrida asks: "What happens when a great thinker goes silent, one . . . whom we read, and reread . . . from whom we were still awaiting a response, as if it would help us . . . to read . . . ?"[21] Derrida speaks here as a reader. The reader was hoping the author would be there to help us, to help us read, to help us understand what is in the text. Upon the death of the author, the reader feels abandoned.

Pronounced at the cemetery, two days after Lévinas's death, these are words of loss, profound loss, a reader's loss. A year later, in "Le Mot d'accueil," speaking again as a reader of Lévinas, Derrida's tone is quite different: "The miracle of the trace . . . allows us to read him today and to hear his voice resonate so it can signify to us" (132, 71).

I am amazed by the phrase "miracle of the trace." Derrida is the great thinker of the trace; there is perhaps no more central idea/image in Derrida's work.[22] For Derrida, the trace is everywhere, always already there. It might even be said that for Derrida there is nothing that is not a trace, there is nothing but traces. Yet this most common and universal thing is here a miracle.[23]

Thanks to the trace—thanks, that is, to writing—we can read Lévinas today. And "today" (aujourd'hui) means in December 1996, after Lévinas has died. Not only can we read him, but we can "hear his voice resonate" (entendre sa voix résonner). The fact that we can read writing is tautological; the fact that through writing we can hear his voice is miraculous. The three words together—"hear," "voice," "resonate"—really insist on the aural quality, making "voice" here seem to be more than just an aspect of writing. The miracle of the trace allows us to hear Lévinas talking to us, today, in the present.

In the French text, the end of the sentence reads: "entendre sa voix résonner pour signifier jusqu'à nous" (literally, "to hear his voice resonate in order to signify jusqu'à us"). The prepositional phrase jusqu'à is difficult to translate: it has a sense of "up to," "until," "as far as," "all the way to." Jusqu'à implies the covering of a noteworthy or even impressive distance; the miracle is in the jusqu'à. The miracle of the trace . . . allows us to . . . hear his voice résonner (reverberate, resound) all the way to us (jusqu'à nous).

What I have just been quoting is from the second paragraph of chapter 4 of "Le Mot d'accueil." The first paragraph of that chapter states, "Lévinas oriented our gazes toward what is happening today," and then lists places where there are refugees, exiled and displaced persons ("from the heart of Nazi Europe to ex-Yugoslavia, from the Middle East to Rwanda . . ."). The point is the political relevance of Lévinas's ethics of hospitality. For my purposes here I want to focus on just one small aspect of this relevance, its relation to time, the fact that relevance is always connected to "today."

"Lévinas oriented our gazes toward what is happening today." We see here the same "today" that will reappear in the next paragraph, but here the main verb is in the past tense ("oriented"). Lévinas in the past directed our gaze to what is happening (present tense verb) today. What we have here in the first paragraph of the chapter is a classic statement of the abiding relevance of a deceased thinker, a dead author. The next paragraph takes this idea of abiding relevance a bit further.

The next paragraph begins: "Emmanuel Lévinas speaks of this. . . . The miracle of the trace . . . allows us today to read him and to hear his voice resonate and thus signify *jusqu'à nous.*" *The second paragraph of the fourth chapter of "Le Mot d'accueil" opens: "Emmanuel Lévinas speaks of this" (Emmanuel Lévinas en parle). Derrida here uses the verb parler ("speak") in the present tense. At Lévinas's funeral, Derrida asked "what happens when a great thinker goes silent [se tait, stops speaking]"; here, a year later, Derrida says, Emmanuel Lévinas parle, "Emmanuel Lévinas speaks."*

:: :: ::

While most of my 2005 memorial for Derrida is either better represented by what has become my second chapter or seems now not worth retaining, I want to hold on to the little bit I have reproduced here. I want to hold on to this idea of the "miracle of the trace" which allows us to "hear" Lévinas speaking, allows him to speak in the present, even after his death. The miracle is that the dead can speak, that the author whose loss Derrida so grieved could a year later speak to him. The dead author who speaks to us is at the heart of the present book. We hear him in chapter 2 when Derrida "turns to the dead for a final word,"[24] and we hear her in chapter 3 when Sedgwick writes in identification with the dead poet. He appears in the first chapter when we look more closely at Barthes's relation to the author, and we find him again at the end of the book when Spivak transforms the dead author into the ghost who "keeps (us) going."

Before moving on there are a couple things I want to remark about the passage I've included from my memorial for Derrida:

(1) The emphasis on the author's voice that I found in Derrida's memorial for Lévinas is surprising because Derrida has famously decried our investment in the voice at the expense of writing (which he called phonocentrism).[25] And it is precisely because what he says runs so counter to our expectations for his relation to the voice that it is so moving. In the way that it counters our received theoretical assumptions, reading Derrida's celebration of the voice here is very much like reading Barthes's desire for the author. Finding passages where such an oft-cited author says something that unsettles received assumptions about what he

thinks may in fact have something to do with hearing a dead author speak. Reading such passages may be a way of releasing him from the categories where intellectual history has buried him. Certainly that is a big part of the project of the present book. It is also central to what I call the ethics of close reading.

(2) In talking about the reader's loss and the miracle of recovering the lost voice in *Adieu*, Derrida is writing about a very particular kind of author, one he calls a "thinker" (*penseur*). Lévinas is such a thinker; so is Derrida. So in fact, I would claim, are all the authors studied in the present book; like Lévinas, they are what we call "theorists." When Derrida asks, "What happens when a great thinker goes silent?" we see that a thinker does not just think but speaks. And when Derrida mourns specifically as a reader, we see that the thinker speaks in writing. Thanks to the miracle of writing it is possible for the thinker to continue to speak after death. A year after Lévinas's death, Derrida asserts: Through the miracle of the trace, we can hear his voice today; the dead thinker speaks today.

I seized on this affirmation of Derrida's because of something I had seen before reading *Adieu*, something I had read shortly after learning of Derrida's death, something that stuck in my craw. A piece in the *New York Times* of October 17, 2004, opens: "With the death on Oct. 8 of the French philosopher Jacques Derrida, the era of big theory came quietly to a close." A few paragraphs later: "Ideas once greeted as potential catalysts for revolution began to seem banal, irrelevant. . . . Deconstruction, Mr. Derrida's primary legacy, was no exception. . . . Today, the term has become a more or less meaningless artifact of popular culture." This article in the *Times*, published a week after Derrida's death, was entitled "The Theory of Everything, R.I.P."[26]

While far from the first declaration that theory was dead and ought to be buried, this one used the occasion of Derrida's literal death to signify a much more total death. The thinker is dead, and so his thought is dead too. His era is yesterday; he does not speak to today. This is precisely what in the present book I am calling theoretical death. And in this *Times* op-ed piece we can see that people connect literal and theoretical death. The present book may have begun in my reading of this article which—however offensive I find the connection there—can stand as evidence of how the literal and theoretical death of the author are entangled.

I read this declaration of Derrida's theoretical death just a few weeks before starting on my memorial. A few weeks after finishing the memorial, I received an advertising circular in the mail. On a sheet dated March 21, 2005, Continuum (a publisher) announced "a new series of books on major thinkers of today": a series they call "live theory." As of the circular, the first four volumes of the series were already out, and they were announcing a fifth one, coming soon, "out this fall"—*jacques derrida: live theory*.

Given what I had read a few months earlier in the *Times*, I was particularly gratified both to read that someone thought theory was "live" and to see Derrida among the "thinkers of today." I kept that circular on my desk; I wanted to hold on to the phrase "live theory." I imagine Continuum meant the series title to convey that these are "thinkers of today" and also to represent the fact that each volume "includes a new interview with the subject." But the phrase meant more to me. Taking it out of context, I felt it represented something I try to do in my reading of theory, something I was trying to do in the book I was writing.

If I were still writing a book on the ethics of close reading, I would want to connect it to this idea of live theory. For me the ethics of close reading has something to do with respecting what is alive, what is living in theory, trying to value theory's life, trying to resist all that deadens it. This involves trying to respect what speaks in theory, to hear the voice speaking. I found an image of that ethics in Derrida's hearing Lévinas's voice, in Derrida's treasuring the voice of the dead thinker. Although this is no longer a book on the ethics of close reading, chapter 2 still lays out my appreciation for Derrida's ethics of reading, for the necessary tension between self and other, the sense of responsibility beyond piety, that I there call the ethics of indecency. And while no longer *on* the ethics of close reading, this remains very much a book *of* close readings. So I need to say that Derrida is not only a source for my ethics of reading, but more centrally the source of my particular practice of close reading.

Although I am sure that many a reader of Derrida would point out the various ways in which my reading practice diverges from his, one aspect of influence is incontrovertible. While Derrida did at times produce readings of poetry and other literary texts, he was by discipline a philosopher and his real innovation was his application of the sort of reading usually applied to literature (e.g., studies of metaphor and image) to writing by philosophers, by "great thinkers." Back in graduate school, reading Derrida gave me license to apply the sort of reading I had been taught to theoretical texts. This sort of reading has sometimes been called reading theory as a literary genre, although I prefer to call it applying literary reading to theoretical texts. While the reading may attend to metaphors and other figures of speech, the author is nonetheless treated as a thinker. In tracing figures and images we are following precisely what we could call thought, or rather thinking—or maybe live theory.

Sometimes reading the liveness of theory means attending to its moment, context, date, temporality. That is an important aspect of my practice of close reading, reading the temporal history of the text, the occasion, the revisions. This means treating theory not as what Spivak in our final chapter calls "once and for all," but as a persistent ongoing practice *in time*. More often it means reading against the monumentalization of theory, the received versions—e.g., Barthes's death of the author, Derrida's critique of phonocentrism—so that the text, the thinking, can come to life again. In such reanimation my consistent move is to focus not on the whole text but on small, striking bits of text. When we stop at such odd bits in a text and ponder them, we are less likely to fall back on received versions that are always based on the main idea. The passages I seize upon tend not to be on the central topic; they point rather toward other theories, other thinking taking place. For example, in a book on the ethics of hospitality and its relation to grave political problems in the contemporary world, Derrida's saying "the miracle of the trace . . . allows us to hear his voice."

While I would want to claim that close reading could make any theory live in this way, the present book reads four theorists whose writing I find particularly lively. These are authors I have taught for decades in order to make theory come to life, in order to show my students the riches close reading can yield. These are theorists I love to read because their writing is full of color and tone, because their thinking is in fact full of voice, because their theory speaks.

::

PART I

::

The Friendly Return of the Author

Chapter 1

::

THE AUTHOR IS DEAD BUT I DESIRE THE AUTHOR

::

In 1992, Seán Burke, writing the definitive study of poststructuralist anti-authorialism, declares Roland Barthes's "The Death of the Author" to be "the single most influential meditation on the question of authorship in modern times."[1] Burke is commenting here, we should note, not on the intrinsic value of Barthes's little essay but on its influence. Although the text in question was just a few pages in a little-known literary quarterly, its title has become a widely familiar, world-renowned slogan.

According to Burke, it is often supposed that "The Death of the Author" was written in the midst of and "in mind of the student uprising" (20). Barthes's essay was published in France in 1968, the year of the nationwide insurrection of students (and workers), and its tone seems perfectly to fit the publication date. Although actually written in 1967,[2] "The Death of the Author" conforms to our image of "1968"—which surely contributes to our sense of the manifesto as historic. The "revolutionary" tone is probably best typified by the text's final sentence: "We now begin to cease being dupes . . . we know that to give writing its future, it is necessary to overthrow the myth: the birth of the reader must be at the cost of the death of the Author."[3]

This sentence is dense with the rhetoric of revolt: We have been "dupes" of a "myth." The moment is "now" to move toward the future and reject ("overthrow") the past. Barthes uses the first person plural and a sort of imperative ("we know it is necessary") to exhort the reader to action. Finally, and most militantly, this final sentence endorses violence as "the cost" of a new future.

If "The Death of the Author" is "the single most influential meditation on authorship in modern times," it is this final sentence which is most often quoted. Actually not the entire sentence (which is longer and more complex than what I have quoted) but the elegant, memorable last clause: "The birth of the reader must be at the cost of the death of the Author." Barthes's polemical essay closes neatly on the five words of its title—a definitive, conclusive, triumphant ending. The last clause of Barthes's manifesto is taken as the definitive statement—not only Barthes's but post-structuralism's—on the question of the author. The author is the past; critics should no longer be concerned with the author; he should be dead to us. The ending is so perfect it has been taken as the last word.

But the militant, elegant slogan is really only the end of a little essay written in 1967. It is in fact not long at all before Barthes brings the author back. In a book published in 1971, Barthes writes: "The pleasure of the Text also includes a friendly return of the author."[4] This sentence appears in the preface to *Sade, Fourier, Loyola*. While "The Death of the Author" might be Barthes's most famous text, especially to those not very familiar with or sympathetic to his work, *Sade, Fourier, Loyola* is one of his least read books. Thus the author dies in an overexposed Barthes and returns in an underexposed Barthes; the imbalance in the reception of these texts tends to obscure the return and exaggerate the finality of the death. And whereas the author's death sounds historic and revolutionary, his return is "friendly." "Friendly" is a far cry indeed from the militant tone of the 1968 manifesto.

While for me "friendly" is the word that jumps out of this sentence from *Sade, Fourier, Loyola*, it is the last four words that are particularly important to Burke, who would elevate "return of the author" to the status of the parallel phrase from 1968. Burke in fact entitles his book on poststructuralist subjectivity *The Death and Return of the Author*; he would replace the familiar catchphrase with this conjunction of two Barthes phrases in order to produce a truer, more accurate representation of poststructuralism's relation to subjectivity. While I am grateful to Burke for making me aware of the "return of the author" in Barthes, my interest in the return is not to find a better definitive figure for poststructuralist theory, but rather to follow the vicissitudes of the dead author in Roland Barthes's writing.

"The pleasure of the Text also includes a friendly return of the author." While the last words of this sentence from *Sade, Fourier, Loyola* give Burke the title to his book, I recognize the first five words as the title of Barthes's next book, published in 1973, one of his best-known works. Although Burke reads *The Pleasure of the Text* for additional evidence of the author's return, what Barthes says there about the author is in fact more peculiar and more evocative: "As institution, the author is dead: his person . . . has disappeared . . . but in the text, in a certain way, *I desire* the author."[5]

The author is dead, Barthes declares again, still in 1973. The author is dead but—nonetheless—I desire the author. This sentence appears in a chapter entitled "Fetish."[6] The standard Freudian analysis of the fetish is that it represents the mother's phallus *even though* we know she has no phallus. We know intellectually that the mother has no phallus, but nonetheless our desire disregards what we know; the fetish represents a solution to the split between what we know intellectually and what we desire. In *The Pleasure of the Text*, a book that affirms the reader's perverse desires, Barthes uses this fetish structure to frame his relation to the author: even though I know he is dead and gone, I nonetheless desire the author.

This is not exactly a "friendly return": fetishistic desire is not necessarily friendly. But both might be opposed to—or outside of—what Barthes here calls "institution," just as both would seem to contrast with the militant, polemical tone of the 1968 essay.

Where Burke settles on the 1971 "return" as the appropriate figure to supplement the overfamiliar "death of the author," I would like in this chapter to follow the various expressions of Barthes's relation to the dead author.

:: :: ::

After "The Death of the Author," the first book Barthes published was S/Z (1970). S/Z has in fact a quite special relation to the 1968 essay. Based on a seminar that Barthes taught in 1968 and 1969,[7] S/Z is an extensive and detailed close reading of the Balzac short story *Sarrasine*. "The Death of the Author," written the year before the seminar, opens by quoting a sentence from the same Balzac story.

After quoting Balzac, "The Death of the Author" proceeds with a series of questions: "Who is speaking thus? Is it the hero of the story? . . . Is it Balzac the individual? . . . Is it Balzac the author? . . . Is it universal wisdom? . . ." The 1968 manifesto then answers the questions with a declaration that goes straight to the essay's polemical point: "It will be forever impossible to know, for the good reason that writing is the destruction of every voice, of every origin" (12, 142).

In S/Z, after quoting the very same sentence from *Sarrasine*, Barthes writes: "The origin of the sentence is indiscernible. Who is speaking? Is it Sarrasine? the narrator? the author? Balzac-the-author? Balzac-the-man? . . . universal wisdom? The crossing of all these origins constitutes writing" (164, 172–73).

The series of questions is similar, with a few variants (for example, "individual" has become "man"). There are enough similarities that this paragraph from S/Z could be considered a revision of the opening of "The Death of the Author." Which would make the difference in the sentence following the questions particularly noteworthy. Both sentences concern the essence of writing (writing is x; x constitutes writing). But, while in 1968 he speaks of writing as "the destruction of every origin," using the rhetoric of violence characteristic of the manifesto, in 1970 writing has become "the crossing of all these origins." In the 1968 essay, this paragraph is followed by one that proceeds to the heart of the essay's topic: "The voice loses its origin, the author enters into his own death, writing begins" (12, 142). In the 1970 book, the paragraph is followed by another, much longer quotation from *Sarrasine*, and then, using this second quotation as the slimmest of pretexts, Barthes devotes a long paragraph to the question of the author. That paragraph begins: "A classical story always gives this impression: that the author first conceives the signified (or the generality) and then looks for . . . signifiers, convincing examples" (165, 173). The paragraph ends by returning to this idea and elaborating upon it: "The *author* is always considered to go from signified to signifier, from content to form. . . . The *mastery of meaning* . . . is a divine attribute, once this meaning is defined as . . . the emanation, the spiritual effluvium overflowing the signified toward the signifier: the *author* is a god" (166, 174, emphasis Barthes's).

S/Z is structured as a series of fragments. Barthes divides the Balzac story into passages of varying lengths, and quotes the entire story in order, piece by piece, commenting as he goes, following each Balzac passage with a short commentary. The order of Barthes's commentaries seems simply to follow the order of whatever occurs in Balzac's text. For example, in the pages just cited, we have a Balzac sentence that leads Barthes to talk about the impossibility of determining who is speaking, followed immediately by a Balzac passage that prompts Barthes to comment on the idea of the author-as-god. We are led to understand that the proximity between these two ideas is arbitrary, suggesting no necessary connection between them, occasioned only by the order of Balzac's text. Yet these same two ideas (the impossibility of knowing who speaks and the author-as-god) are in fact both found in the 1968 essay "The Death of the Author," which also quotes the first of these two Balzac fragments. (The second of these two fragments, I might add, has only the slightest possible relation to the author-as-god idea that Barthes derives from it.) The juxtaposition of these two ideas thus seems more than arbitrary.

Near the middle of "The Death of the Author," Barthes writes: "We know now that a text is not made of a line of words, releasing a unique, sort of theological, meaning (which would be the 'message' of the Author-God)" (15, 146). While this parenthetic remark is the single mention in the essay of the "Author-God," it is absolutely central to Burke's reading: "This co-implication of the writer and divinity . . . tacitly expatiates and enlivens Barthes's essay" (23).[8] This co-implication is, according to Burke, informed by a "homology": "The author is to his text as God, the *auctor vitae*, is to his world" (23). While this homology is only "tacit" in "The Death of the Author," we can see a more explicitly articulated version in the commentary from *S/Z* that comes almost right after the one paragraph in the book that clearly derives from the 1968 manifesto.

While the "Author-God" appears but once in "The Death of the Author," as the essay progresses it increasingly uses a capitalized "Author" rather than the lower-case "author" with which it begins (ending, as we know, "the birth of the reader must be at the cost of the death of the Author"). I read this capitalized "Author" as a version of the doubly capitalized "Author-God."[9] More centrally, the entire essay equates the author with God by putting the author in God's place in the Nietzschean slogan "God is Dead."

Barthes returns to the topic of the author-as-god near the end of *S/Z*: "The Author himself—the somewhat decrepit deity of the old criticism—can, or could some day, become a text like any other: we will only need to renounce making his person . . . the origin . . . whence would derive his work" (200, 211). The "Author," capitalized as in the 1968 essay, is here explicitly equated with a "deity." Yet, however the worse for wear, this god is not in fact dead. The author-as-god is again, as earlier in *S/Z*, the origin whence flows the work, but if we could renounce that version of the author, then the decrepit old guy need not die but can rather "become a text."

According to Foucault, in modern times writing underwent a historic reversal that transformed it from bringing immortality to killing the author.[10] I wonder if we see here in *S/Z* another turn of that screw: if the author can "become a text," then, like a classical hero, he need not die. Barthes hesitates as to whether this is possible in the present ("can") or only in the future ("or could some day"). The passage continues with future-tense verbs, seeming to decide that this transformation of the author must wait for the future, but it is worth noting that, at least for an instant, Barthes seems to think it already possible.

Burke considers this passage from *S/Z* to be "the annunciation" of "the return of the author" (48). While the use of future tense verbs here definitely makes it some sort of announcement, I want to remark that the author here is not dead but only decrepit, and that while there is indeed a "return" in this passage, it is a different sort of return: "The Author himself . . . could some day, become a text . . . we would only need to give up making his person . . . the origin . . . we would only need to consider him himself as a paper being and his life as a *bio-graphy* (in the etymological sense of the term) . . . the critical enterprise will then consist in *returning* the documentary figure of the author into a novelistic figure" (200, 211, emphasis Barthes's).

Barthes uses and emphasizes the word "return" in this passage, but the return here is not a return from the dead, but a return from documentary to novel, from nonfiction to fiction. This is in fact a rather strained use of the verb "return"; the combination of strain and emphasis suggests Barthes may be troping on the return. We see the strain particularly in the odd phrase "returning into," a phrase which takes the transformation of "turning into" and marks it as a repetition—suggesting that this future transformation will bring us back to an earlier (more original) state.

This idea of the author as "novelistic figure" will take on increasing resonance in later books by Barthes, and we will return to it. I would like here also to remark the other word that Barthes emphasizes (and strains?) in this passage: "bio-graphy." Barthes hyphenates the word to make us see the "writing" in "life-writing." In *Sade, Fourier, Loyola*, published just a year after *S/Z*, he will in fact experiment with a new kind of author biography. In the prefatory note to that book, he will once again use and italicize this hyphenated spelling, referring to the "principles of *bio-graphy*" that he followed.[11] These gestures that will be picked up in later books bear out Burke's sense of this passage as an "annunciation" and give specific resonance to the future tense of its verbs.

The passage from the end of *S/Z* that we have been slowly reading literally ends on the names of two authors: "The Author himself . . . could some day, become a text . . . the critical enterprise (if one can still speak of criticism) will then consist in *returning* the documentary figure of the author into a novelistic figure . . . a task whose adventure has already been recounted, not by critics, but by authors themselves, such as Proust and Jean Genet" (200, 211–12). This passage moves from "The Author himself" to "authors themselves," not only from capitalized to lower-case, but from singular to plural. The passage is in fact all one sentence, and in the course of this sentence (a very long sentence, to be sure) we move from the Author that we are beyond to authors that are beyond us, as if the sentence itself enacts the turn in Barthes's relation to the author. And as we reach this new relation to authors (lowercase, plural), Barthes names two examples: Proust and Jean Genet.

While "The Author" belongs to the past ("decrepit," *vétuste*, timeworn), the "authors"—despite being historical figures—belong to the future. Past and future here are not literary but critical. "The Author" belongs to the old criticism; the "authors" are models for the criticism of the future. The task envisioned for future critics has "already been" achieved by these authors; it has already been "recounted," i.e., narrated; the model for criticism is narrative, novelistic. Proust and Genet both wrote autobiographical novels, novels woven out of the material of their lives, and thus are named here as models for our future relation to the author. This is for Barthes a serious model: after *S/Z*, his criticism (if one can still call it that) will become increasingly autobiographical.

We might be surprised to see the author of "The Death of the Author" celebrating two authors by name, taking on the sort of humble, laudatory relation to them that would seem to betoken a more traditional relation of critic to author, seeing their achievements as far beyond anything accomplished by critics. While the admiration puts the critic in a classically secondary position, the idea of the author as model imagines a future in which the critic could do what these exemplary authors have done (something which thus might no longer be called "criticism").

As it turns out, Proust and Genet return, likewise paired together, in *The Pleasure of the Text*, published three years after *S/Z*. This time the two authors appear not as models for criticism but as examples of "figuration." Declaring that we must distinguish between "figuration" and "representation," Barthes explains what he means by the former term: "Figuration would be the way the erotic body appears in the profile of the text. For example: the author can appear in his text (Genet, Proust), but not in the guise of direct biography (which would exceed the body). . . . Or again: one could conceive a desire for a character in a novel" (88–89, 55–56).

Genet and Proust are examples of authors who appear in their texts. They figure in the text in the same way as a character in a novel (the other example he gives); they appear in the text in the way Barthes prefers (Barthes dislikes representation, likes figuration). In the words of *S/Z*'s announcement, in the case of Genet and Proust, the author has "returned into a novelistic figure." We can recognize here the word "figure" from *S/Z*, as well as novelistic, but there is also something else in the 1973 book—the figure of the author is not only novelistic, it is sexy. The author appears in the text as an "erotic body," like a character for whom we might "conceive a desire." In the erotic context of *The Pleasure of the Text*, might the pairing of Genet and Proust signal not only the autobiographical novel but also a shared identity as homosexual authors?

Whether or not their homosexual identity matters, Genet and Proust function in this 1973 book as objects of Barthes's desire. The passage where they appear in parenthesis as exemplary erotic figures leads us back to the passage from this same book that earlier I quoted briefly: "As institution, the author is dead . . . but in the text, in a certain way, *I desire* the author: I need his figure, (which is neither his representation nor his projection)" (45, 27, emphasis Barthes's). This specification of the "figure" as neither a representation nor a projection is not explained further until the passage dozens of pages later where Barthes defines figuration. Barthes desires the author, *in a certain way*; he not only desires him, but he *needs* him. He needs his "figure"; he needs his "erotic body" appearing, in a certain way, in the text, appearing in a way that will arouse Barthes's desire. And the examples given of that appearance, of the author appearing "in a certain way"—in the same way as a character, in a way that Barthes finds erotic—are Genet and Proust.

As institution, the author is dead, but that hardly means Barthes does not care about, does not feel anything for the author. On the contrary, Barthes desires the author. In the wake of the dead author, Barthes outlines an erotic relation to the author. In our contemporary critical vocabulary we might want to call such a relation to the author queer; in the language of the 1973 *Pleasure of the Text*, we would call this anti-institutional, anti-normative erotic relation perverted, or perverse.

:: :: ::

Between *S/Z* (1970) and *The Pleasure of the Text* (1973), Barthes published one book, a book whose title names three authors (one of whom is nearly synonymous with perversion)—*Sade, Fourier, Loyola* (1971). While not nearly as well known or as often read as *S/Z* or *The Pleasure of the Text*, this book is in fact absolutely central in articulating Barthes's relation to the author.[12]

The most striking and unusual feature of Barthes's 1971 book is how it ends. After four essays—one on Fourier, one on Loyola and two on Sade—there is a final section entitled "Lives." In it we find a ten-page "Life of Sade" and then a two-page "Life of Fourier"; both lives are numbered lists of anecdotes and details from the authors' biographies. There is no "Life of Loyola," because, as Barthes tells us in a prefatory note, he "couldn't write this Life in conformity with the principles of *bio-graphy* alluded to in the preface" (16, 11).

This book's preface contains, I believe, not only Barthes's "principles of *bio-graphy*," but also his longest theoretical consideration of the author outside the 1968 essay. We might note that, in the very process of "alluding to" his principles for writing an author's life, Barthes also happens to refer to Proust (who this time appears without Genet). Barthes says, "A life . . . like Proust was able to write his own in his work" (13, 9): as it was at the end of *S/Z*, Proust's autobiographical novel is here again, still the model.

I would like now to proceed with a slow, detailed reading of the penultimate paragraph in the 1971 preface, which is the paragraph where Proust appears and where Barthes refers to his "principles of *bio-graphy*." The paragraph opens with a short, simple sentence, which I have already had occasion to quote: "The pleasure of the Text also includes a friendly return of the author." The next two sentences elaborate directly on the return of the author: "The author who returns is certainly not the one who has been identified by our institutions. . . . The author who comes from his text and goes into our life has no unity: he is a mere plural of 'charms,' the site of a few tenuous details, yet a source of vivid novelistic glimmerings . . . this is not a (civil, moral) person, this is a body" (12, 8). There is an interesting specification of the return here. The "author who returns" is the "author who comes from his text and goes into our life." The author returns from the world of the text to life, but if the return is a return from the dead, the life returned to is not the author's but our life. The author returns to us.

We see in this passage a few of the themes we have already considered—the novelistic author, the anti-institutional, the move from the singular to the plural. In addition here, however, is the "friendly" which, as I remarked earlier, does not seem to gibe with the sexual perversion of the very book announced in the first five words of this passage. Yet when we look at the third sentence of this passage, we find that "the friendly return of the author" does ultimately involve "a body."

Whatever Barthes means by "friendly" here (*amical*, amicable), it connotes a relation not to the person but to the body. The "friendly" is opposed to the institutional; it is also opposed to the "person" because the "person" for Barthes is a civil or a moral entity, and thus an institution. The person is singular ("has unity"); the body is plural ("charms"). In *The Pleasure of the Text*, the author's body is explicitly an erotic body; here in this passage from the earlier book, which points to that 1973 book, the author's body is not explicitly sexual, but rather plural, charming, and friendly. This plural body is the nonnormative body; it is, I would argue, the perverse body.[13] The "friendly," whatever it might exactly mean, is part of the perverse relation to the author that Barthes is formulating.

There is actually something else in this passage, something I left out upon first quoting it, something I find particularly significant for my reconsideration of "The Death of the Author": "The author who returns . . . is a simple plural of 'charms' . . . a source of vivid novelistic glimmerings . . . in which we nonetheless read death more surely than in the epic of a destiny; this is not a (civil, moral) person, this is a body" (12, 8).

Not only does the author return here, but so does death. If the author is a body, then he is mortal. In the very passage where he declares the return of the author, Barthes also seems to be reflecting on, adding meaning to, the death of the author. Burke notices this: "Where the death of the author had addressed itself to the timeless 'Author-God', the return of the biographical author is a return to transcience [*sic*], mortality" (39). Or, as he says later, "We notice that the return of the author came to be associated with the mortality of the author, just as 'The Death of the Author' never took account of the author as anything other than a strange deist abstraction" (60). Burke repeatedly notices this, but he does not examine this odd chiasmus any further. I find myself fascinated and puzzled by the fact that, whereas in "The Death of the Author" the author is the sort of abstraction that never lives and thus actually cannot die, the author who returns is a mortal body and thus poignantly subject to death.

Among other things, we might observe that there are considerations of literary genre here: Barthes contrasts the novelistic with the epic. Note that the contrast is not between epic and novel, but between the heroic genre and the "novelistic." Where the novel can, like the epic, trace a "destiny," the novelistic is that plurality of details that exceeds the singularity of a destiny. (The singularity of destiny is about the "civil, moral person.") While we might associate "death" with the arc of a destiny, the hero's tragic or glorious *telos*, Barthes says we "read death more surely" in the plural of details that betoken the body.

The passage we have been considering (the first three sentences of the paragraph) is followed by a long sentence that gives examples of the specific "charms" Barthes finds in the lives of the three authors of the book's title: "What comes to me from Sade's life . . . is not the solemn contemplation of a destiny, it is, among other things . . . his white muff when he accosted Rose Keller . . . what comes to me from Fourier's life is . . . his death among the flowerpots; what comes to me from Loyola are not his pilgrimages . . . but only 'his beautiful eyes, always a little filled with tears'" (12–13, 8).

I would like to note a couple things in this sentence. (1) We find here again the word "destiny," which we already saw in the previous sentence. Barthes contrasts the "solemn contemplation of a destiny" with Sade's white muff: the former is singular and epic, the latter novelistic. "Destiny," which will appear again in the last sentence of the paragraph, betokens the traditional way of representing a life; it consistently stands for what Barthes's new way of doing biography is writing against. (2) This sentence also includes the word "death." Fourier's "death among the flowerpots," while literally an author's death, seems a far cry indeed from "The Death of the Author." This novelistic death is sweet, touching, poignant.

After this sentence giving specific examples from the lives of the three authors, the paragraph's final sentence returns to the general theorization of the author: "If by a twisted dialectic there must be in the Text, destroyer of every subject, a subject to love, that subject is dispersed" (13, 8–9).

Even though the paragraph is explicitly about the "return of the author," here in the paragraph's final sentence, Barthes repeatedly uses the word "subject" rather than "author." In the parlance of the time, "subject" (short for "speaking subject") was the appropriate theoretical term for whomever in the text is speaking. We might remember that "The Death of the Author" begins with the question "Who is speaking?" Foucault's "What is an Author?" similarly begins with the question "What does it matter who is speaking?" The term "subject" appears prominently in Goldmann's response to Foucault: "The negation of the subject is today the central idea of a whole group of thinkers" (Foucault 813). Two years later, Barthes uses this abstracted, dehumanized theoretical term for the author—but he uses it in order to put in greater relief the surprising twist he is wringing on the current theoretical orthodoxy.

In this final sentence of the paragraph we also find some of the violent rhetoric that was in his 1968 manifesto: the Text (capitalized here in the 1971 preface as the Author was in 1968) is a "destroyer," bringing death to every subject. But despite this, there is still, "there must be" in the text "a subject to love." Despite its destruction of the author, the text must contain an author to love. Barthes calls the logic that, despite the death of the author, gives us an author to love a "twisted dialectic"—we might also call it a perverted dialectic. Or we might call the love for the author thus a twisted love.

The subject we love in the text is "dispersed": we recognize here the theme of the absence of unity, the plurality of the author. Barthes then adds an association, as if by chance, to this idea of dispersion: "If . . . there must be in the Text . . . a subject to love, that subject is dispersed, a bit like ashes thrown to the wind after death (to the theme of the *urn* and the *stele*, strong, closed objects, instructors of destiny, would be opposed the *bursts* of memory, the erosion that leaves nothing of the past life but some furrows)" (13, 8–9).

This dispersion, this mode of existence that characterizes the author, is likened—but very lightly ("a bit like"), as if merely a chance association—to ashes strewn after death. Barthes then adds a parenthesis that elaborates on the seemingly chance association, thus strengthening the funerary dimension that emerges as a digression within a digression (a parenthetic comment occasioned by a chance association) but instead ends up a dominant insistence. The parenthesis begins by citing an "urn," which contrasts directly with strewing ashes (after a cremation, the ashes can either be strewn or kept in an urn). But then the urn is paired with a "stele" as two solid objects meant to memorialize the dead, and those two objects are together contrasted with the volatility of memory.[14]

(We might again note the word "destiny," which we have already seen twice in this paragraph. Here "destiny" is associated with the solid, lasting kind of memorial, which in this instance is the wrong relation to the dead author. A "stele" is a stone with an inscribed surface used as a monument. Connecting this use of "destiny" with its first appearance in the paragraph places the stele on the side of the epic and in opposition to the novelistic and suggests that, although the stone's solidity is meant to ensure that the commemoration will be read, we might, ironically, "read death *more surely*" [emphasis added] in the dispersed furrows left by memory.)

While we have already found so many ideas and resonant images in this sentence that begins with the "twisted dialectic," it is far from over. This sentence—the last sentence of the paragraph—is in fact incredibly long, spanning twenty lines of the text.[15] Of the many things included in it, by far the most stunning is the turn Barthes makes immediately after the parenthesis contrasting the stele with bursts of memory: "If there is in the Text . . . a subject to love, this subject is dispersed, a bit like ashes . . . after death (to the theme of the *urn* and the *stele* . . . would be opposed the *bursts* of memory): . . . if I were a writer, and dead, how I would love it if my life were reduced, by the treatment of a friendly and casual biographer, to a few details" (13, 8–9).

Barthes shifts here to the first person singular and to an imagined conditional—"if I were . . . how I would. . . ." From theorist of the text ("if there is in the Text a subject, this subject is dispersed"), he shifts (within the same sentence) to imagining himself as a writer. Not only as a writer, but as a dead writer. The connection between writing and death is here so strong that to imagine being a writer is, almost immediately, coupled with imagining being dead. There is something evocative and eerie, something quite perverse, about the fantasy. In the fantasy he would be dead, but not beyond feeling: "If I were a writer, and dead, how I would love it . . ." Barthes imagines the pleasure he would feel as a dead writer.

If he were a dead writer, he would love to have his life "reduced to a few details." Earlier in the same paragraph Barthes writes that the "author who returns . . . is . . . the site of a few tenuous details." In the beginning of the paragraph he is theorizing the place of the author in the reader's pleasure; here he turns to imagining that same place as what would give the author pleasure, that is, give the dead author pleasure. By means of putting himself in the place of the dead author, Barthes imagines something that would give pleasure to both reader and author, imagines a pleasure they might share.

This reduction of the dead writer's life takes place, in Barthes's fantasy, by means of "a friendly and casual biographer." In this book, Barthes is himself a casual biographer who reduces the lives of dead writers to a few details. If Barthes were a dead writer, he would want to be under the treatment of the very sort of biographer that he in fact is. The word "friendly," so striking in the first sentence of the paragraph ("friendly return of the author"), returns here. Whatever the word "friendly" is supposed to signify in this paragraph about the return of the author, note that it is here coupled with "casual" (*désinvolte*).

"If I were a writer, and dead, how I would love it if my life were reduced, by the treatment of a friendly and casual biographer, to a few details, to a few tastes, to a few inflections, let us say: some 'biographemes,' whose distinction and mobility could travel outside any destiny and come to touch . . . some future body" (13, 9). Barthes here coins the word "biographeme" for the small, particulate units that he composes into lists in order to make the "Lives" at the end of the book. This word which he first uses here in this 1971 preface will stay with him, reappearing in his 1975 autobiography, *Roland Barthes par Roland Barthes*, and in his last book, *La chambre claire* (1980). About this coinage, Burke comments: "As the morpheme is to the linguistic analysis, the mytheme to myth, so the biographeme is the minimal unit of biographical discourse. Yet despite these scientific consonances . . . it is a poet's conception" (38). Or, I would say, a novelist's. Just as Barthes would separate the novelistic from the novel, he would separate the biographeme from the biography. Where the biography, like the novel and the epic, recounts a destiny, the "biographeme" "could travel outside any destiny."[16]

While the "biographeme" is crucial for understanding Barthes's "principles of *bio-graphy*," and while it will continue to play a role in his later work, I want here to focus not on what the biographeme is but rather on what, in this sentence where it first makes its appearance, it does. The biographeme, traveling "outside any destiny," *comes to touch some future body*.

This connection between the biographeme and the ability to touch will reappear in Barthes's last book, which is about photography and is centrally concerned with death ("there is in every photograph the return of the dead").[17] In that book Barthes likens photographs to biographemes: "I like certain biographical features which, in the life of a writer, enchant me like certain photographs; I have called these features 'biographemes'; the Photograph has the same relation to History as the biographeme has to biography."[18] And, like the biographemes in the 1971 preface, photographs in Barthes's last book can reach across time and produce an uncanny bodily touching: "From a real body, that was there, are sent radiations that come touch me, me who am here

. . . the photo of the disappeared being comes to touch me" (126, 80–81). The time travel which in the 1971 book involves "some *future* body" is here represented by the touching between the past tense "that *was* there" and the present tense "me who *am* here."

Death is central and poignant in *La chambre claire*, a book written in mourning for his mother's recent death. It was my familiarity with that book, in fact, that made me query the militant, triumphant way he talks about "death" in "The Death of the Author" and thus was part of what led to the present chapter. If my goal were to reach a full understanding of Barthes's relation to death, I would want to spend a good deal of time looking at *La chambre claire*, but for my purposes here I want instead to remain with the peculiar fantasy in the preface to *Sade, Fourier, Loyola*.

"If I were a writer, and dead, how I would love it if my life . . . could come to touch some future body." Barthes's fantasy ("if I were . . . how I would love it") ultimately involves touching a body; Barthes fantasizes that after he is dead, he will nonetheless be able to touch a body. In this fantasy death need not mean the end of one's ability to touch bodies. As Foucault reminded us in "What is an Author?," before the modern turn we call the death of the author, writing was thought to bring immortality. Barthes, through another turn of the trope, gives back to the writer a kind of immortality, not the heroic, monumental immortality of the person, but a bodily immortality, an ability to touch bodies after death.

Barthes used the word "body" once before in this long paragraph we've been reading: "The author who returns . . . the author who comes from his text and goes into our life . . . is not a person, it's a body." When we put this "body" (the author as body) together with the later body ("some future body") — after Barthes has twisted his speaking position from living reader ("our life") to dead writer — we end up with bodily contact between the author and the future reader.

It is this possibility of the author's body coming to touch some future (reader's) body that Barthes calls "the friendly return of the author." Whatever he means by "friendly," it characterizes a relation that is bodily and casual. (I find myself thinking of "casual sex," "friendly sex," and wondering if there is a gay or a queer coloration to this friendly return of the body.)[19] We have here a sort of immortality—a bodily, erotic immortality—a fantasy, a desire, a bodily touching that extends beyond death. This bodily immortality is not, however, an overcoming of death but some other relation to death: "The author who comes from his text and goes into our life . . . is a simple plural of 'charms,' the site of some tenuous details . . . in which nevertheless we read death more surely than in the epic of a destiny; it is not a (civil, moral) person, it is a body." The relation we have to the author who comes from his text into our life is a bodily relation, and it is because it is a bodily relation that "we read death more surely." The "epic of a destiny" is about the "person," but the civil, moral person is a sublimation of death; it is the body that dies.

The urn and the stele, lasting monuments, are, as Barthes puts it, "instructors of destiny." They maintain solidity, unity; the only immortality they grant is one that has no body, no touching, no life. They are, Barthes says, "closed objects"; they hold things in; they do not allow dispersion; they do not allow anything to "travel outside of destiny"; they do not allow anything of the dead out to "come touch some future body." The author as institution, the author taught by literary history, is a monument, an epic destiny; that author cannot touch us. But Barthes imagines another author, a friendly body, a mortal author, who even after he is dead, can "come touch some future body."

The long final sentence of the paragraph we've been reading from the preface to *Sade, Fourier, Loyola* does not end on the "future body." Barthes's fantasy of being a dead writer occurs about halfway through the sentence. The sentence goes on to cite Proust, and then to discuss intertitles in silent films, and finally comes back around to an exemplary biographeme from each of his three authors, ending thus: "Sade's white muff, Fourier's flowerpots, Ignatius's Spanish eyes" (13, 9). While the sentence goes on, my slow, detailed reading will stop here.

The sentence and the paragraph and the preface go on (this is not the last but the second to the last paragraph of the preface). Where I am stopping is not in fact even the end of a clause. The clause with Barthes's fantasy, the clause where he introduces the "biographeme" actually ends: "some future body, promised to the same dispersion" (13, 9). This return to the generalized dispersion of the subject is to me so much less interesting—touches me, moves me so much less—than the fantasy of some future body; it represents a return to the theoretically correct Barthes. I want to stop right here so that, rather than following Barthes's exposition of theoretical principles, we can linger with his extraordinary and perverse fantasy: *"If I were a writer, and dead, how I would love it if my life . . . could travel outside any destiny and come to touch . . . some future body."*

:: :: ::

This fantasy, as it appears in *Sade, Fourier, Loyola*, specifically concerns not the author's writing but his life. While the future body touched may be a reader, he is not reading the writer's work but rather his biography. I find myself compelled by this fantasy, however, not because of what it says about biography, but because I glimpse in it some version of the relation between reader and author, because I take it to be a slightly twisted, somewhat displaced fantasy of a reader's connection to the author. Keeping this fantasy of bodily touching in mind, I want for the rest of the chapter to look specifically at places where Barthes sketches a reader's relation to the author.

Let us begin by recalling that this very paragraph where Barthes fantasizes being a dead writer who touches a body actually includes an articulation of the reader's relation to the author. Two sentences before the fantasy, we read: "The author who comes from his text and goes into our life . . . is a body" (12, 8). Here we are talking not about the author's biography but "his text." The author "comes from his text"; the text is not a "closed object," the author can travel outside of it into our life. The first person plural here implies readers; those who have contact with the text and thus can receive the author in "our life." When the author comes into the reader's life, he is a body.

This idea of the author coming "into our life" is discussed at some length in the paragraph that precedes the one we just spent so long reading:

> The Text is an object of pleasure. . . . often only stylistic. . . . At times, however, the pleasure of the Text is achieved in a more profound manner . . . when the "literary" text . . . transmigrates into our life, when another writing (the Other's writing) manages to write fragments of our own dailiness, in short when there occurs a *co-existence*. The index of the pleasure of the Text then is that we can live with Fourier, with Sade. Living with an author . . . is a matter of making pass into our dailiness fragments . . . from the admired text (admired precisely because it scatters well). (11–12, 7, emphasis Barthes's)

Barthes uses the verb "transmigrate" for this passage from the text into our life. Transmigration is a passage after death into another body. In a transmigration we usually assume only one exists — the other is dead and gone when the transmigration happens — but in this transmigration, there is a "co-existence" (the word Barthes emphasizes in this passage); the two bodies exist together (even though one is dead). "Co-existence" is Barthes's term for "living with" — a phrase he repeats after announcing the co-existence. I hear the "life" in "living with" (life in contrast to death), but I also hear something else, something cozier and more domestic, which makes me want to replace Barthes's more abstract "co-existence" with "cohabitation." The idea of cohabitation picks up on the "dailiness" of this relation. Living with an author is having him be part of our daily life.

Living with an author is having "fragments" from his text in our dailiness. Barthes specifies that we admire a text because "it scatters well"[20] (like ashes strewn to the wind). A text can scatter well precisely because it can be broken into fragments which, like the biographeme, have "the distinction and the mobility to be able to travel." There is a connection for Barthes between the "fragment," the small unit, and the ability of the author to "travel," to leave his text and come alive in our life. Barthes's books from this period are composed of fragments—short little sections with no connective tissue between them—as if he wants to optimize the possibility that they can travel into readers' lives. My reading here is also very fragmentary although my fragments are not exactly cut out along the same lines proposed by the text. My reading breaks the text into pieces that resonate for me, breaking off those pieces of the text that are for me today most alive with meaning.

In the passage that I just quoted at length, I would like finally to note the insistence on otherness. This transmigration involves what Barthes calls "an other writing" (*une autre écriture*); to make sure we give weight to the otherness of that writing, he repeats and reorganizes the phrase in parenthesis as "the Other's writing" (*l'écriture de l'Autre*). This co-existence is a relation to an other, or an Other—a relation to otherness; the relation to the author is a relation to otherness. The reader's pleasure is more profound when through reading an other enters our lives, comes to live with us.[21]

In this passage from the 1971 preface, Barthes twice uses the phrase "the pleasure of the Text."[22] The passage thus points us to Barthes's famous little 1973 book, in which we find further delineated the reader's relation to the author as other. Barthes introduces the author into *The Pleasure of the Text* thus: "Lost in the middle of the text (not *behind* it like a god of machinery) there is always the other, the author" (45, 27, emphasis Barthes's). The French word for author (*auteur*) is quite similar to the French word for other (*autre*). The appositive juxtaposition at the end of this sentence ensures that we see the resemblance and makes the two terms almost interchangeable, nearly identical. The author is the other; the author is the other *in* the text.

Reading is a relation to the other; the other is "always" there. Whereas our usual practice is to understand the other as "behind" the text, Barthes insists that the other is "in" the text. The other who would be "behind" the text would be like a "god of machinery," a *deus ex machina* pulling the strings. The author "behind" the text is the Author-God, but the author as other, far from pulling the strings, far from being in a position to control the text, is not only in the text but *lost in the text*.

I find this idea of the author as "lost in the text" very evocative. Not only does it suggest an author in the text but not in control, it also suggests the author might want to but cannot get out of the text. That idea, of the other who is as if trapped in the text, might be related to the idea from *Sade, Fourier, Loyola* of the author who comes out of his text and into our lives. The image of the author "lost in the text" could also suggest that he is there but the reader cannot find him, cannot reach him. If the relation to the author is a relation to an other, it is a relation to an other who is always there but always lost, who cannot be discounted but cannot be reached.

Lost in the middle of the text, there is always the other, the author. We find this statement in a little fragment/chapter composed of two paragraphs. The first paragraph ends on this image of the author lost in the text; the second paragraph opens: "As institution, the author is dead." When Barthes writes "there is always the other, the author," this must be thought together with the death of the author. The "always" thus pointedly contrasts with, belies, the idea of some end to the author, of the author as no longer with us.

I have already quoted the second paragraph of this particular fragment — twice, in fact — in the present chapter. This paragraph is where I found my chapter title. I would like to return to this paragraph one more time, to consider it again. Among other reasons, this time I want to reconsider it in relation to the image of the author as lost other, an image that appears in the paragraph, in the sentence, immediately preceding it.

"Lost in the middle of the text . . . there is always the other, the author./ As an institution, the author is dead: his . . . person has disappeared."[23] "Disappeared" here seems to be another way of saying "dead," gone, but when we consider its proximity to the preceding paragraph, "disappeared" also resonates with "lost." The author's person is not simply gone but has disappeared into "the middle of the text."[24]

"As institution, the author is dead: his . . . person has disappeared . . . but in the text, in a certain way, *I desire* the author" (45–46, 27). Barthes italicizes the phrase "I desire"; his emphasis here is on his desire, and on the subjective articulation (first person singular) of that desire. Reading this sentence, I myself would instead emphasize its "but." I want to emphasize how his desire is in tension with the author's death, in tension with the disappearance of the author as person. "But" means "on the contrary"; "but I desire" suggests the contrary or perverse nature of his desire.[25]

We find a similarly perverse desire articulated by D. A. Miller when the object of Miller's desire happens to be Roland Barthes. Miller tells us that he seeks an "opportunity" for "intimacy" with Barthes, and then, self-conscious about the perversity of this desire, he adds: "Barthes, of course, is some ten years dead, *but* who could ever think . . . that someone's death ever stopped the elaboration of someone else's fantasy about him?"[26] Miller's "but" here in 1992 is, I would say, very close to Barthes's 1973 "but": Barthes is dead *but* . . . ; the author is dead *but*. . . .

While strikingly parallel to Barthes's contrary desire, Miller's formulation also, parenthetically, contains something else: "But who could ever think—in particular, at this date, what gay man—that someone's death ever stopped the elaboration of someone else's fantasy about him?" Writing in 1992, Miller connects this perverse desire-despite-death to gay men. The context, of course, is the AIDS epidemic and the way death had, in the ten years since Barthes died, become so imbricated with gay male sexuality.[27] But despite this particularity ("in particular"), Miller also gestures toward a more generalized perversity ("but who could ever think?"). By using the term "perverse," or "perverted," in this chapter, I hope to connote something like what I find here in Miller's sentence: a more general logical perversity (e.g., Barthes's "twisted dialectic") with parenthetic shades of anecdotal gay particularity.

"As institution, the author is dead . . . but in the text, in a certain way, *I desire* the author" (45–46, 27, emphasis Barthes's). Despite the death of the author, despite the institution, Barthes insists on his desire for the author. He underlines "I desire"; I have been emphasizing his contrary "but." In this assertion of his desire, I would like, now, finally, also to note the phrase "in a certain way." Might there be a shade of gay particularity in Barthes's declaration that he desires "in a certain way"? More generally, could we not define perversion as desiring-in-a-certain-way? Specifically, I would say that this chapter has been an attempt to trace that "certain way"—to trace the way that Barthes desires the author.

Lost in the middle of the text, there is always the other, the author.

The author is dead . . . but in the text, in a certain way, I desire the author.

Chapter 2

THE ETHICS OF INDECENCY

::

. . . if I were a writer, and dead . . .
—Barthes, 1971

In 1980, Roland Barthes was hit by a truck and died. The next year, Jacques Derrida published an essay entitled "The Deaths of Roland Barthes."[1] This memorial for Barthes, respectful and earnest as it might be, could also be said to constitute a sort of infidelity. It brings Derrida to break a promise, a longstanding promise: "What long ago . . . I had promised myself never to do . . . was to write *upon the death . . . upon the occasion of the death*, in gatherings . . . of writings 'in memory of' those who when alive would have been my friends, present enough to me that . . . some analysis or 'study' would seem to me . . . strictly intolerable."[2]

In 1981, on the occasion of Barthes's death, Derrida writes his very first text "in memory of," his first memorial essay. In this memorial, Derrida tells us that he found such writing, on such an occasion, "strictly intolerable." That he had "long ago" vowed, promised himself, never to do exactly what he is doing. We learn of this promise as he is breaking it: "What long ago . . . I had promised myself never to do (out of a concern for rigor, for fidelity, if you like [*si l'on veut*])." Briefly, parenthetically, Derrida tries to explain this promise as a concern for rigor or, rather, what he imagines the reader might prefer to call (*si l'on veut*) "fidelity." While we might imagine this as concern about loyalty to his departed friend, it is actually a question of fidelity to himself, to the promise he made himself. Barthes's death might have made Derrida betray himself.

"The Deaths of Roland Barthes" is an analysis of two of Barthes's books. This is precisely what Derrida vowed never to do: write an analysis or a study of a friend's work on the occasion of his death. What Derrida found "strictly intolerable" were writings that combined mourning and study or analysis. Perhaps not coincidentally one of the books Derrida is writing about itself combines mourning and analysis. (Barthes's last book, *Camera Lucida*, is both a study of photography and a work of mourning for his recently departed mother.)

Although Barthes was a friend, by writing an analysis or a study, Derrida is treating him as an author. The passage which reveals his broken promise, the passage about how such writing is intolerable, appears in fact as part of a discussion of relations to the "author." Derrida gives us a "brief classification" of the different temporal relations readers can have to authors: (1) "The 'author' can be already dead"; (2) "authors living at the moment we read them"; (3) "And then there is a 'third' situation: upon the death and after the death of those we have also 'known,' met, loved, etc." (76–77, 49). Derrida finds the first two relations relatively easy; the third is the one he finds intolerable—the relation where someone passes, moves from the category of the living to the dead. What is really troubling is neither the living nor the dead author but precisely what we might call the death of the author. Since this talk of authors and the question of whether they are dead or alive takes place in an essay on Barthes, I cannot help hearing the phrase "the death of the author" hovering around this passage.

Neither in this passage on authors and death nor anywhere else does the essay entitled "The Deaths of Roland Barthes" mention Barthes's notorious 1968 manifesto. (Perhaps this is because what in a United States context may be Barthes's best-known essay was not such an important text in the French context.) While it does not so much as mention "The Death of the Author," I nonetheless find in Derrida's memorial for Barthes a contribution to the theorization of the author's death. I would like here to read that contribution, thus continuing my reconsideration of the death of the author.

Here is how Derrida introduces his typology of relations to the author: "There are, in the *time* that relates us to texts and their signatories . . . three possibilities" (76, 49). Note that Derrida italicizes the word "time." This is a theorization of the author with an insistence on temporality, on the moment of reading: "living *at the moment* we read them." In Derrida's memorial for Barthes, I find a rethinking of the death of the author that makes it inextricable from the fact of reading in time.

As Derrida lays out the three different relations to the author, the difference marks the very terms of his exposition. *(1) "The 'author' can be already dead"; (2) "authors living at the moment we read them"; (3) "And then there is a 'third' situation: upon the death and after the death of those we have also 'known,' met, loved, etc."* I am not sure why already-dead authors are authors-in-quotes whereas living authors are not in quotation marks, although I find that difference evocative. (How is being dead like being in quotation marks? Does the term *author* imply a living person?) What I want most to remark here, however, is the complete absence of the term *author* from the third situation (or rather the "third" situation). When talking about this third possibility, he uses neither author nor author-in-quotes but only the pronoun "those."

This seems particularly noteworthy because he does this exact same thing again. After outlining the classification, Derrida immediately applies it to his own experience: "Thus: I have had occasion to write about . . . texts whose authors were dead long before I read them or whose authors are living at the moment I write. . . . But what . . . I had promised myself never to do . . . was to write *upon the death* . . . of those who when alive would have been my friends" (77, 49–50).

Here we have the same three possible relations, in the same order, not this time an abstract classification but documenting Derrida's own experience. He uses the word "author" twice (without quotation marks) for the first two temporal relations, but the word "author" does not appear in the third situation. Even though this is clearly a typology of relations to the author, it is as if he cannot bear to use that word in the third temporality, the moment of passing, the moment of death. *Upon the death of* . . . : it is as if Derrida cannot bear to say "the death of . . . the author." Instead, he again uses the pronoun "those" and then proffers the word "friends."

When first presented, Derrida's classification seems to involve any reader's relation to the author, but as Derrida goes on to apply it to his own experience, he reveals that what he is really thinking about is not just any reader, but in fact a particular kind of reader, a reader who is writing about his reading. This typology thus involves not only a temporality of reading but the moment of writing, a temporality of writing, as well: "I have had occasion to write about . . . texts whose authors were dead long before I read them or whose authors are living at the moment I am writing" (77, 49).

Derrida's three possibilities are all variants of one particular relation—the relation to the author of a reader who is writing about his reading. This of course is what Derrida commonly does, throughout his work: in other words, he is locating his essay on Barthes in relation to a lifetime of writings based in readings. This allows us to see that while the typology separates the memorial essay from other readings Derrida has published, it also connects them. This relation to the author, this writing which is reading, is what we generally call criticism (we might also call it analysis or study). It is this particular relation that seemed to him intolerable upon the death of his friends: to write about his friends' texts, to treat his friends as authors.[3]

In 1971, Barthes proposed that the author's death would be followed by "the friendly return of the author."[4] While I never have been quite sure what Barthes meant by "friendly," I wonder if that might not be what we see here in Derrida's 1981 memorial: Derrida finding himself forced to read the dead friend as author, forced to think the dead author as friend. While for Barthes the friendly return of the dead author opens onto an erotic relation, for Derrida the death of the author friend is experienced most sharply in the ethical register.

:: :: ::

In "The Deaths of Roland Barthes," Derrida confesses: "What I believed impossible, indecent, unjustifiable, what . . . I had promised myself never to do . . . was to write *upon the death* of . . . those who when alive would have been my friends, present enough to me that . . . some analysis or 'study' would seem . . . strictly intolerable."

Quoting this passage earlier, I focused on the broken promise and on what exactly Derrida found intolerable: I requote it now in order to add the series of adjectives that introduces the passage, adjectives where I find the mark of an ethical reaction. I am particularly interested in the adjective in the middle because it might provide a connection between Derrida's ethics and Barthes's erotics, but also because in the context in which I read Derrida's memorial for Barthes, the context of its 2003 republication, the word "indecent" becomes particularly salient.

Derrida first published "The Deaths of Roland Barthes" in the journal *Poétique* the year after Barthes died. He published it again in 1998, in a collection of his essays entitled *Psyché*. Not having read it in either of those venues, I first encountered this memorial to Barthes when Derrida published it as the lead essay in his 2003 volume *Chaque fois unique, la fin du monde* ("Each Time Unique, The End of the World"). This 2003 book with the evocative title is a collection of short texts published over the course of twenty years—each one, like the memorial for Barthes, written on the occasion of the death of a friend of Derrida's. While Derrida in 1981 tells us he finds such writing "impossible, indecent, unjustifiable," that is nonetheless exactly what he does, for the first time on the occasion of Barthes's death, but then at least 15 more times, in the next two decades, as we see collected in *Chaque fois unique, la fin du monde.*

Issued by Derrida's usual publisher, Galilée, in a series that Derrida edits with three colleagues (a series that includes many of his other books), this 2003 collection might appear to be a typical book by Derrida. However, as he tells us in the foreword, this thick volume is a "strange artifact"; as it says on the back cover, "This work appeared first in English, in the United States (The University of Chicago Press, 2001)."

While it seems wonderfully fitting, to be sure, that the "original" of a Derridian book should already be a translation,[5] I am in this case more interested in the reasons Derrida gives for why this particular book appeared in English first. In the foreword (which was written especially for the French edition), Derrida tells his French reader: "I would never have dared to take the initiative for such a collection in France, in 'my' country and in 'my' language. . . . The position of survivor that such a collection seems to display would remain for me in 'my' language . . . intolerable. Indecent, even obscene" (9–10). Although we might note the quotation marks around "my" here as indices of Derridian distancing from the idea of a pure origin (that is, the native language in which one is originally at home), I am more interested in the three-word sentence fragment at the end of this passage. In French such a collection would be, he tells us, "intolerable" (we have seen him likewise use "intolerable" in the Barthes memorial). Here in the foreword he follows "intolerable" with a sentence fragment that dwells on how wrong such a collection would be, stringing out a sequence of three adjectives, presumably in order of increasing offensiveness—intolerable, indecent, obscene. There is that adjective "indecent" again, and once again it plays the middle position in a series of three adjectives.

While the addition of "obscene" here strengthens the connections between Derrida's ethical considerations and Barthes's erotics, I want to focus on the median adjective "indecent": it will recur with some insistence in and around this book, and it has a particular resonance in this passage. The verb Derrida uses to say what such a collection would seem to do (the verb I have translated as "display") is *exhiber*, which not only can mean display or flaunt, suggesting an unseemly showing off, but is also the verb used for the obscene display that in English we call indecent exposure. As Derrida prepares the book for publication in French, prepares the French reader for what is to come, he warns us that he finds such a book indecent. More than twenty years earlier, as he wrote the very first of the essays in this book, he likewise confesses that he finds such writing, on such an occasion, indecent. I want to keep an eye on this gesture, this repeated gesture, and its peculiar ethical posture.

:: :: ::

Derrida tells us that he "would never have dared take the initiative" of such a publication in France. While he has indeed already published the individual pieces in France, it is their collection together into a volume that turns them into this unseemly display. At least that is what he says here, in the 2003 foreword.

One of the texts included in this collection is the short speech Derrida delivered at Emmanuel Lévinas's funeral. Spoken at the cemetery in December 1995, just two days after Lévinas died, that speech was first published in 1997 as part of a book by Derrida entitled *Adieu à Emmanuel Lévinas*. The prefatory material to this book informs us in regard to that short speech: "Such words, so quickly wrenched from sadness and from the night, we would never have dared publish them if the initiative had not first been taken in the form of a little book edited in Athens, in Greek, by Vanghelis Bitsoris."[6] Let me note in passing that the problem with this text, why the editorial we "would never have dared publish" it, seems connected to something being "so quick." These words are unseemly, embarrassing (belonging to the night and not the light of day) because they came so quickly. There is, as I hope to have the time to show later in this chapter, a problem with precipitation, with the "too fast" that threads through *Chaque fois unique*.[7] But for now I only want to note the striking similarities between this warning in *Adieu* and the remark in the 2003 collection. Derrida writes in the foreword to *Chaque fois unique*, "I would never have dared take the initiative"; six years earlier, in the opening to *Adieu*, "we would never have dared publish them if the initiative hadn't first been taken."[8] In both 2003 and 1997, Derrida tells us he is doing something he "never would have dared" to do; in both, what he wouldn't have dared to do is take the initiative; in both, the initiative comes from someone else; and in both instances his text is published in another language before it is published in French.

The similarity between these two passages suggests that Derrida's sense of impropriety is not just, as he says in 2003, about collecting the mourning pieces together. At least in the case of Lévinas, it was about publishing it at all, or to be more precise about taking the initiative to publish it. Somehow he can do what he never would have dared to do if following someone else's initiative.[9] What makes it possible, in both these cases, to do what he would never dare, is not only following others' initiative, but also passing his text through another language. "Adieu," the speech Derrida delivered at Lévinas's funeral, is first published in Greek in 1996; before its French publication, "Adieu" is in fact published not only in Greek but twice in English as well.[10] "Adieu" was translated into English by Pascale-Anne Brault and Michael Naas; the very same Brault and Naas are the initiators of the collection that becomes *Chaque fois unique, la fin du monde*.

In the foreword to *Chaque fois unique*, Derrida says: "The position of survivor that such a collection seems to display would remain for me in 'my' language . . . intolerable. Indecent, even obscene." The sentence fragment ends a paragraph; the next paragraph begins: "And yet, I believed I should accept this proposition." The paragraph begins with a conjunction, a sort of enjambment in prose; this is a new paragraph but also linked, continuous with the preceding. *Intolerable, indecent, obscene; and yet. . . .* The peculiar ethical posture here involves recognizing, even emphasizing, not denying or covering up, the indecency of a gesture and doing it nevertheless. *Indecent, and yet.*

"And yet, I believed I should accept this proposition: that . . . Michael Naas and Pascale-Anne Brault, whose project and whose incomparable labor it is, take responsibility for an American edition. . . . This book is thus *their* book. . . . I hold them to be, I insist upon it, the true authors of this work" (10).

Although his name appears on the cover and title pages in the position of the author, Derrida "insists" in the foreword that Michael Naas and Pascale-Anne Brault are the "true authors of this work."[11] While he wrote the texts, theirs is the "proposition," the "project," the "initiative," the "responsibility." True authorship here is not writing, it seems, but initiating and being responsible.

Immediately following Derrida's foreword is a prologue by Brault and Naas that gives the word "author" quite a different meaning. Talking about the "bio-bibliographical notices" that appear at the end of the collection, they tell us that Kas Saghafi "prepared the biographies and the bibliographies of the *authors* Derrida talks about in this book" (13, emphasis added). Brault and Naas use the word "author" several times in their prologue, always, as here, to refer to the subjects of Derrida's writing, to Derrida's deceased friends. At one point they put "authors" and "friends" in apposition, equating the two terms: "*Les auteurs, les amis américains de Jacques Derrida* [the American authors, friends of Jacques Derrida] . . . are little known . . . to the majority of French readers" (13). This apposition of author and friend goes, I would say, to the very heart of the book. In each text in this collection, Derrida is writing about a friend, expressing his friendship, but at the same time he is writing about an author; in each, he talks about the friend's writing, quotes the writing, talks about reading, and exhorts us to read his friend. In each case, I would say he treats his deceased friend as an author and at the same time treats the dead author as a dear friend.

I am hoping in this chapter to examine at length *Chaque fois unique*'s particular equation of author and friend, to investigate what it means to treat one's dead friends as authors. I want to read *Chaque fois unique* as a theorization of the author in the wake of the author's death—a reconceptualization of the "death of the author" so as to include personal loss—perhaps even as a version of the friendly return of the dead author, foretold by Barthes.

I want to return to what Derrida says in the foreword about the two people he insists are the "true authors" of the book: "I believed I should accept this proposition: that other friends, Michael Naas and Pascale-Anne Brault whose project and whose incomparable labor it is, take responsibility for an American edition" (10). Naas and Brault are not only, for Derrida, authors; they are friends. The proposition he accepted is specifically that "friends take responsibility" for publishing this writing of his. Having written about his departed friends, Derrida would have found it intolerable to display these writings if other friends had not taken the initiative and the responsibility. Somehow it is the proposition coming from friends, the book being not his alone, but his being in it with friends that makes what would have been intolerable tolerable. "I thought I should accept this proposition: that other friends, Michael Naas and Pascale-Anne Brault . . . take responsibility for an American edition, under the title *The Work of Mourning*." The original American edition is in fact entitled *The Work of Mourning*; the proposition initiated by Brault and Naas would seem to include that title. Derrida accepted the proposed title, and he goes on here to gloss its terms in relation to Brault and Naas: "This book is thus *their* book, above all the *work* of both of them. A work where the intensity of emotion, the discrete refinement of shared mourning compromise with an audacious labor (*travail*) of knowledge, an authentic *scholarship*" (10). Insisting in particular on the word "work," Derrida distributes the American title's two nouns: the mourning is his; the work is theirs. This strange artifact is a "compromise" between their work (labor, scholarship) and his mourning (intensity of emotion, discrete refinement).

Nowhere in the French book does it say why the collection's title was changed. Since I've begun working on this book of

Derrida's, I have had the repeated experience, upon mentioning the French and English titles, of hearing an immediate and decided preference for the French title, by one friend or another who had not previously heard of the book. Certainly the French title is more poetic. It also more clearly expresses the irremediably contradictory nature of these texts, setting up a logical tension between "each time" and "unique." The English title does not immediately suggest that there is a tension between mourning and work—a tension Derrida gestures toward in the foreword by using the phrase "compromise with": "A work where the . . . emotion, the . . . mourning *compromise with* an audacious labor of knowledge" (emphasis added).

The Work of Mourning is a less evocative, more theoretical title. It is undoubtedly apt: in these texts, Derrida frequently talks explicitly about the psychoanalytic concept of the work of mourning, and often uses that phrase (*le travail du deuil*). When he uses the phrase, however, he generally expresses suspicion and distance in regard to it. For example, in the speech delivered at Lévinas's funeral, included as the penultimate chapter of *The Work of Mourning*, Derrida speaks of "that confused and terrible expression 'the work of mourning'" (242, 200). Brault and Naas translated this funeral address in 1996; later that same year they conceived the idea of a book they would call by this very same "confused and terrible expression."

In what context does Derrida call "the work of mourning" a "confused and terrible expression"? Two days after Lévinas's death, speaking at the cemetery, Derrida remarks that "often those who make themselves heard in a cemetery end up addressing themselves *directly*" (emphasis in original). Derrida, who will himself end up speaking directly to Lévinas, goes on to explain why we do this: "It is . . . because all language that would come back towards . . . us would seem indecent, like a reflexive discourse that would return toward the stricken community, toward its consolation or its mourning, toward what is called, in that confused and terrible expression, 'the work of mourning'" (241–42, 200).

If we do not speak to the deceased, then we speak only to ourselves, we speak only for ourselves, to console ourselves. We speak only to begin the work of mourning. In this context, speaking just two days after the death of his friend, such a discourse, consoling and mourning, "would seem indecent." Not only is the expression "the work of mourning" confused and terrible, but the thing it names, in this context at least, seems indecent.

And yet . . . Derrida would never have dared publish these words he spoke so soon after Lévinas's death. But—thanks to the initiative of another, via the mediation of another language—these words were published. Derrida would never have dared collect such texts into a book, but—thanks to the initiative of other friends, via the mediation of another language—he agreed to have this very speech not only collected but included under the sign of "the confused and terrible expression 'the work of mourning.'"

Indecent, and yet . . . while I might be tempted to reject the title of the American edition, citing as evidence Derrida's seeming distaste for the expression, tempted to dismiss it as Brault's and Naas's and instead embrace the French title as the real thing, the real Derridian thing, more evocative, less crude, I think that would be missing the point of the very particular practice I am glimpsing here. A practice that is at once extremely sensitive to indecency but nonetheless does not attempt to remain decent and pure. While we might want to connect this to a general Derridian project of deconstructing purity, we see the ethical stakes of this, I think, most acutely in these texts written in response to the death of friends.

Brault and Naas, the initiators of this collection, themselves directly address what I am here calling the ethics of indecency. In their introductory essay to the volume, we can find the word "indecent." For example, they write: "At the death of a friend, we feel it is almost indecent to speak, and yet. . . ."

I cut Brault's and Naas's sentence in the middle so you would see the structure "indecent, and yet." Or in this case, *almost* indecent, and yet. The sentence continues: "and yet the substitution of the name for the body, of the corpus for the corpse, appears to be the only chance the dead have left" (52, 28).[12] *Almost indecent, and yet the only chance.*

The idea of substituting "the name for the body, the corpus for the corpse," draws on the terms of Derrida's essay on Sarah Kofman in the volume. In that essay, Derrida reads the text Kofman was working on when she died, an analysis of a painting by Rembrandt. The painting depicts a corpse surrounded by doctors who rather than looking at the corpse only have eyes for the book laid open between its legs. Derrida's and Kofman's texts are both wonderfully rich,[13] but for my purposes here, I will say only that Derrida connects the doctors' preference for the book ("corpus") over the corpse with what he and his readers are doing "right here in this moment" (217, 176), "what we are doing . . . when we write or read books, when we speak of a book, in place of the other" (222, 180). Substituting the name for the body, the corpus for the corpse means speaking of the other's writing when the other is dead, treating the dead friend as an author (the author is a "name" and has a "corpus").

"At the death of a friend, we feel it is almost indecent to speak, and yet the substitution of the . . . corpus for the corpse appears to be the only chance the dead have left. That is why Derrida so often cites the dead in these texts and, near the end of so many of them, turns to the dead for a final word" (52–53, 28). *Almost indecent, and yet the only chance.* In these texts, Derrida regularly quotes, and often at length, from the published writing of the friend who has died. Brault and Naas locate the impetus to quote within the peculiar ethics of indecency; I want here to consider Derrida's practice of quoting in these texts.

"Near the end of so many of [the memorial texts, Derrida] turns to the dead for a final word." While Derrida quotes liberally throughout these texts, Brault and Naas draw our attention especially to a particular gesture. For example, Derrida begins the final paragraph of his speech at Louis Althusser's funeral, "And now I want to turn it over to him, to let him speak. For another last word," and ends by reading aloud a paragraph from Althusser's *Pour Marx* (150, 118). Likewise, in a text written for a memorial service in honor of Joseph Riddel, the final paragraph begins, "I would like, in order to conclude, to give back or leave the word to Joe—his word," and ends with a quotation from Riddel's *The Inverted Bell* (167, 132).

While the published translations here are quite different, in fact Derrida uses the exact same phrase, *rendre ou laisser la parole*. The translations differ primarily because of the word *parole*, a word rich in meanings, which corresponds to a number of different English words. *Parole* means both "word" and "speech": its usage here is close to how we might talk about, for example, a debate where we can *prendre la parole* (literally take the *parole*, i.e., speak) or *passer la parole*, hand it over, to someone else. The phrase Derrida uses, *rendre ou laisser la parole*, means to give (him) back or to let (him) have *la parole*, the floor, as we say. As he ends, Derrida wants to cede the floor to his dead friend, to stop speaking about him, and let him speak. He hesitates as to whether this would be giving the floor *back* (*rendre la parole*) or simply giving it to him (*laisser la parole*). I'm intrigued by Derrida's hesitation between the two verbs (*rendre ou laisser*), especially because he repeats this particular phrase, as if in its specificity it gets at something particular he wants or needs to do when speaking upon the occasion of the death of a friend.[14]

I would like to look more closely at these instances of giving his friend the last word, these sites that Brault and Naas signal as exemplary of Derrida's ethical bind. I too find these passages exemplary but I find them also surprisingly dense and ethically very complex. After saying he wants to give Althusser the last word, but before he actually reads the paragraph from Althusser's book, Derrida explains his choice of quotation: "Rereading him yesterday evening, and late into the night, this imposed itself on me" (150, 118). A dear friend has just died; it is the night before the funeral where Derrida will speak, and he is rereading the friend's published writings. In this collection we often find him thus rereading his friends just after they have died.

"Rereading him yesterday evening, and late into the night, this imposed itself on me rather than my reading it — or electing to say it again here." Although he tells us he was "rereading" Althusser, he curiously claims that he did not "read" the passage he is about to quote. Rather than "reading" or choosing to quote this passage, relations in which he would be doing something to the text, Derrida insists upon his passivity and the text's active, even imperious, relation to him: "This imposed itself on me." There is actually something a bit spooky about this scene: while in the evening he is rereading, doing something very familiar, late into the night something different happens — the text takes possession of Derrida, turns him into a vessel through which Althusser can speak.

While I am fascinated and indeed moved by this story of a late-night mutation of the reading relation, at the same time I cannot help but note that this imposition by the text on Derrida sounds in fact like something he says in the memorial for Barthes about his customary relation to the texts he writes about: "The 'author' can already be dead . . . at the moment we begin to read 'him,' *indeed when this reading orders us to write* . . . second possibility, authors alive at the moment we are reading them, *indeed when this reading orders us to write*" (76–77, 49, emphasis added).

"Indeed when this reading orders us to write": Derrida uses this strange, striking phrase twice in his discussion of the three temporal relations to the author. He uses it twice, identically, of the first two possible relations, a dead or a living author. Derrida does not use this phrase for the third possibility, does not mention being ordered to write in relation to an author who has just died; however, this idea of the text commanding the reader appears in the 1981 essay for Barthes right as Derrida prepares to reveal his sense of the indecency of writing about an author who has just died. Perhaps there is a connection between that indecency and this sense of being ordered to write. In any case, whatever the connection, this idea that the reading orders us sounds in some way like Derrida's experience a decade later reading Althusser the night before his funeral.

Rereading him yesterday evening, and late into the night, this imposed itself on me rather than my reading it. What is reading that Derrida would insist he was not "reading" on such an occasion? Rendered no doubt especially acute by the occasion—by the rawness of the friend's death, perhaps by reading "late into the night"—the nature of reading seems itself at stake here. Hearing his claim that the text he quotes "imposed itself on" him as echoing "when this reading orders us to write" in the Barthes memorial, I would specify that what is at stake is the particular practice of writing-based-in-reading (Derrida's lifelong practice—and ours too). I would add that this practice generally involves quotation.

In claiming that he did not read nor choose the quotation, Derrida would present it as coming as directly as possible from Althusser, without mediation. The wish to efface himself and let the other speak is strong in these memorial texts, repeated, insistent. Brault and Naas cast Derrida's gesture as an example of the politics of mourning. While it is undoubtedly and movingly that, I find it also richly if mysteriously evocative as an example of an ethics of quotation. "In a first moment," write Brault and Naas in their introduction, "citation seems to be a way of avoiding the indecency or irresponsibility of speaking simply *of* the dead, *of* them as subject or object. Whence the possibility of simply citing them, of letting them speak without interference or interruption" (46, 23).[15]

It is indecent to speak of the dead, to turn them into objects in our discourse; the decent thing to do would be to let them speak. Quotation would seem to be a way of avoiding "indecency or irresponsibility." Brault and Naas link indecency and irresponsibility here; I however would not link these two in this way. I find rather that Derrida connects indecency not, as we might expect, with irresponsibility but with responsibility. I would argue that while quoting "without interference or interruption" might well be a way to avoid indecency it is also a way of avoiding responsibility.[16]

In a first moment, quotation seems to be a way of avoiding indecency. My insistence on "in a first moment" gestures toward the fact that the ethics of quotation negotiates a temporal dimension. What in a first moment might avoid indecency could become, in another moment, indecent. What I am calling the ethics of indecency must necessarily grapple with this effect of temporality.[17]

In a first moment, quotation seems to be a way of avoiding indecency, and yet . . . Just a year after he says he wants to give Althusser the last word, Derrida will likewise say, using the identical phrase, that he wants to give Riddel the last word. Derrida will then introduce the actual quotation from Riddel thus: "With the awareness of sacrificing, I am cutting one more piece, hastily, out of . . . *The Inverted Bell*" (167, 132). Although just a few brief words, the violence here is striking: the idea of sacrifice resonates with the verb *découper*, which means to carve, to cut up,[18] and there is the additional violence of haste. (So often in these texts, there is a sense of haste as violence.)

If "in a first moment," quotation seems to be a way of avoiding indecency, in another moment we are faced with what Derrida calls "the violence of quotation." In the first essay of the collection, the memorial for Barthes, as he is introducing a long quotation, Derrida declares: "We should not be able to quote but I take upon myself the violence of quotation, and above all of a quotation necessarily truncated" (89, 59). We carve out quotes, cut up the text, *découper*; a quotation is "necessarily truncated"; such truncation is the inescapable violence of quotation. Derrida here takes the violence upon himself, takes responsibility for the violence. While Derrida may not avoid indecency here, he does avoid irresponsibility. It is this taking of responsibility, this particular combination of violence and responsibility, that I am here calling the ethics of indecency.

Derrida's declaration of "the violence of quotation" appears in the memorial for Barthes, in his first ever memorial essay, as he is about to quote, not from the dead friend who is the subject of this essay, but from another friend, still living, Maurice Blanchot—as Derrida is about to quote from an essay called "Friendship" that Blanchot wrote on the occasion of the death of his friend,

Georges Bataille. Derrida is writing for the first time in a new genre, a genre he vowed never to write in, and he takes Blanchot's memorial essay for Bataille as his model, his precursor text.[19]

As Derrida prepares to quote from Blanchot's memorial for Bataille, he wants to be sure we know how very wrong what he is about to do is: "From these few pages . . . we have no right to take anything for ourselves. What ties Blanchot to Bataille was unique. . . . And yet, the metonymic force of even the most poignant writing allows us to *read* these pages" (89, 59). Here once again we find the ethics of the "and yet." We have no right to take anything for ourselves; and yet, we can read these pages. What is in Blanchot's memorial for Bataille belongs to them not to us. And yet . . . Derrida italicizes the word "read" here: what we have no right to do, and yet what we are doing is, in a word, read.

The genre that Derrida found impossible, indecent, unjustifiable to write is the same genre he says here that we have no right to read. These two indecencies are in fact the same one. Derrida found it impossible to write on the occasion of the death of the author precisely because such writing would be read. What allows us to read is "the metonymic force of writing"—the fact that writing creates unintended connections, does not stay bound to context. (This seems a classically Derridian sense of writing.) Regardless of the unique and poignant context, this is still writing, and thus can be read in other contexts. The word "unique" in this passage resonates with the book's title. Just as the title gives us the contradiction of a repeated "unique" (*Each Time Unique . . .*), "the metonymic force of writing" allows for the repetition of the unique in other contexts.[20]

"We have no right to take anything for ourselves," the paragraph begins. The same paragraph ends: "We should not be able to quote but I take upon myself the violence of quotation, and above all of a quotation necessarily truncated." The violence of quotation is connected here to something quite indecent about reading, at least in the context of these memorial texts. Expressive of something poignant and unique, these texts can nonetheless be read by anyone, by those who don't know, don't understand, don't feel, don't care. They do not belong to us, we have no right to them; we should not be able to quote, but we can. Derrida tells us this as he is about to quote.

In the first essay in *Chaque fois unique, la fin du monde*, Derrida declares emphatically that we have no right to quote, takes responsibility for the violence of quotation, and then goes on to quote at some length from Blanchot's memorial for Bataille. Derrida will quote from this same little Blanchot essay again, more than two decades later, in what will become the very last memorial in *Chaque fois unique*, his 2003 speech at the cremation of Maurice Blanchot. That the collection should end with an homage to the man who wrote the text Derrida takes as a model for the genre gives the book a certain satisfying sense of completion. (Perhaps that is why it was at this moment, right after Blanchot's death, that Derrida decided to publish the collection in French, in his language, in his country.)

The Blanchot memorial is, however, not included in *The Work of Mourning*, which appeared two years before Blanchot's death. Instead, the 2001 American edition ends on an essay in honor of Jean-François Lyotard, and, in this essay too, we find Derrida grappling with the violence of quotation. Written for a memorial gathering in 1999, the essay is a close reading of a text by Lyotard and includes a good number of long quotations. About two-thirds of the way through the essay, Derrida says, by way of introducing a block quote, "In the few lines that I should not have the right to isolate in this way, I wanted to underline . . ." and then follows a list of things he wanted to emphasize about the text (278, 232). The language here echoes what he wrote in his first memorial essay before quoting Blanchot. In 1981: "We should not be able to quote"; "We have no right to take anything for ourselves." In 1999: "I should not have the right to isolate."

The text on Lyotard refers to quoting as isolating a few lines; saying he should not have the right to quote, Derrida goes on to quote. He then follows that quotation immediately with another quote, or rather, almost immediately. Derrida first interjects a short parenthesis: "And further on (but I am suffering so much from the necessity, for lack of time, of not reading everything . . .)" (279, 232).[21]

Derrida follows one long quote almost immediately with another ("And further on"), but as much as he is quoting, it is not nearly enough. He is suffering from not being able to quote the entire text, "everything." The "necessity of not reading everything" reminds me of his saying, in the first essay of the collection, that quotation is "necessarily truncated." In that first essay, Derrida took responsibility upon himself for the necessary truncation; in the last essay he tells us he is suffering so much from the same necessity. As we here follow Derrida's ethics of quotation, I want to think that responsibility together with that suffering. "(But I am suffering so much from the necessity, for lack of time, of not reading everything in order to hurry toward a certain posthumous '*nous*')." "Reading" here actually means quoting. Derrida is suffering from not having the time to quote Lyotard's entire text; he can't quote everything because he is hurrying, trying to get somewhere. (Note, in passing, haste again causes suffering.) What he is trying to get to is where Lyotard talks about the pronoun *nous* (first person plural pronoun, equivalent of "we" and "us"). He is trying to get to where Lyotard says, "We are only 'us' posthumously." (Lyotard's little sentence is intriguing, and I'm afraid I do not have time here to consider what Derrida says about it because, ironically, I want to focus on the violence of quotation.) Derrida's essay is in fact entitled "Lyotard and *nous*," and is a meditation on the "posthumous 'us.'" Derrida is hurrying to get to the part of Lyotard's text that he makes central to his own reading, and he suffers on account of that hurrying, but he does it nonetheless.

For lack of time, Derrida cannot "read" the entire text; so in order to quote, he must do violence to the text, cut pieces out of it. This violence of quotation, what twenty years earlier he calls truncation, is here in the essay on Lyotard called isolation: "the few lines that I should not have the right to isolate this way" (278, 232). A little earlier in this essay, Derrida connects quoting with leaving Lyotard alone: "The first desire would be to let Jean-

François speak, to read him and quote him, him alone, getting out of the way, but nonetheless without . . . leaving him alone, which would be another way of abandoning him" (270, 225). I want to connect the "isolate" that Derrida in this essay uses for the *découpage* of quotation with this idea of leaving alone or abandoning. These two different aspects of the violence of quotation echo each other in "Lyotard and *Us*."

In this quote, Derrida speaks of letting Jean-François speak, letting his dead friend speak, using again the phrase we saw at the end of his memorials for Althusser and Riddel. Derrida's first impulse is to let Lyotard speak, which he would do by reading and quoting. This gesture of letting him speak involves Derrida getting himself out of the way so Lyotard would speak without interference. The problem is that this gesture would leave Lyotard alone, it would isolate him.[22]

Recall Brault's and Naas's formulation in the introduction: "In a first moment, citation seems to be a way of avoiding the indecency . . . of speaking simply *of* the dead. . . . Whence the possibility of simply citing them, of letting them speak without interference or interruption" (46, 23). This is very close to what Derrida says here about Lyotard: "In a first moment," "the first desire," "letting them speak without interference" "quoting him, him alone, getting out of the way."

In a first moment this seems to be a way of avoiding indecency, but "the first desire would be to let Jean-François speak, to read him and quote him, him alone, getting out of the way *but nonetheless* without . . . leaving him alone, which would be another way of abandoning him." The "him alone" of quoting him alone becomes the "him alone" of leaving him alone. Quoting without interference or interruption isolates the dead friend, abandons him. It seems to me that the "us" is very much at stake in the question of leaving the friend alone while letting him speak. Abandoning the friend, leaving him alone, isolating him, is a breach of the "us."

Speaking at a memorial gathering for Lyotard, a year after his death, Derrida says: "I wanted . . . to avoid an homage in the form of a personal testimony . . . which always risks giving in to that indecent way of saying 'us,' or worse, 'me,' there where the first desire would be to let Jean-François speak, to read him and quote him, him alone . . . but nonetheless without . . . leaving him alone, which would be another way of abandoning him" (270, 225).

Brault and Naas see quoting without interference as a way of avoiding the indecency of talking about the dead friend; here in his memorial to Lyotard, Derrida sees quoting without interference as a way of avoiding a somewhat different indecency, the indecency of talking about oneself, saying "me." What both indecencies share is that of the survivor talking rather than ceding the floor to the dead friend.

The indecency here is, however, not just saying "me," but "saying 'us.'" There is an indecent way of saying "us," the pronoun that is the subject of this very essay. Whether Derrida manages to avoid the indecency, whether he succeeds in saying "us" in a more decent way—perhaps by saying it in quotes, perhaps by quoting Lyotard saying "us"—I'm not sure. But I am interested in the way the final essay in *The Work of Mourning* centers on a word that, in this context at least, carries the risk of indecency.

It is the articulation of this risk of indecency that brings Derrida to the ethics of quotation:

> I wanted . . . to avoid . . . a personal testimony . . . which always risks giving in to that indecent way of saying "us" . . . there where the first desire would be to let Jean-François speak, to read him and quote him, him alone . . . but nonetheless without . . . leaving him alone, which would be another way of abandoning him. A double injunction, thus, contradictory, and without mercy. How to leave him alone without abandoning him? (270–71, 225)

How to leave him alone without abandoning him? This can sound like a question about mourning, and it surely is, but in this context it is also a question about the ethics of quotation.

Derrida quotes Lyotard with a sense of "injunction," ethical imperative, moral law. The injunction must be followed, but the injunction is contradictory. And without mercy. No wonder he suffers so much while quoting. This injunction without mercy brings Derrida to the place of responsibility and suffering.

Derrida has in fact on another occasion articulated a very similar sense of a double law apropos of quotation. While the text in question was not included in *Chaque fois unique*, it belongs to the same genre as the writing in that volume.[23] Lecturing about Paul de Man's work in 1984 just a few months after de Man's death, Derrida reflects on the practice of quotation on such an occasion: "At the limit of fidelity . . . a discourse 'in memory of' . . . could be content to quote. . . . Out of fidelity, one ought to quote in the desire to let the other speak (again) but one should not, one should not be content to quote. It is with the law of this double law that we are here engaged."[24] Here we see once again the desire to let the other speak (and Derrida here uses the exact same phrase we saw at the end of his memorials for Althusser and Riddel). And, as in the memorial for Lyotard, this desire leads to a double injunction.

"This double law" is a law about quoting, about "being content to quote" (*se contenter de citer*), about limiting oneself to quoting, about being content to contain oneself, to quote without commentary. The extreme of fidelity would content itself with quoting, but "one should not, one should not be content to quote." The force of the law is perhaps best heard in that repeated "one should not," as if the repetition of the prohibitive formula itself embodied the doubleness of the law. The actual "law of this double law" is, like the double injunction in the text on Lyotard, articulated around the conjunction "but": one ought to quote *but* one should not be content to quote.

The ethical imperative here is, perhaps, one should not be content. There is in this idea of *se contenter de*, of contenting oneself with, not only the problem of complacency, but the question of containment, limitation. And in fact an explicit problem of limitation actually accompanies the first occurrence of *se contenter de citer* in the passage, in a phrase that above I elided for simplicity: "at the limit of fidelity . . . a discourse 'in memory of' . . . could be content to quote, *supposing one knew where to begin and how to stop a quotation*" (emphasis added).

The problem with "simply" quoting is that a quotation is not a simple thing. Even if we do not interfere, interrupt, or comment, we still decide where the quotation begins and ends. The phrasing here is in fact striking and not parallel: Derrida literally says "supposing one knew where to begin and how to stop a quotation." The wording "how to stop a quotation" suggests something hard to get under control. And indeed one of the things we see in these memorial texts is Derrida piling quote upon quote, as if having trouble stopping. In the short piece on Gilles Deleuze, for example, Derrida quotes a few sentences from Deleuze's *Logique du sens*, and right after closing the quote, he places a parenthesis: "(One would have to quote interminably)" (235, 192). A few years later, in the essay on Lyotard, Derrida, while adding long quote to long quote, will parenthetically bemoan that he could not "read everything." Quotation is necessarily truncated; even the most faithful quotation must do violence.

But even supposing one knew how to stop a quotation, we would, however, nonetheless still be engaged with the law of the double law. In the 1984 lecture in memory of de Man, after revealing the double law of quotation, Derrida announces the ethics of his engagement: "One ought to quote in the desire to let the other speak but one should not, one should not be content to quote. It is with the law of this double law that we are here engaged. . . . I thus must quote but also interrupt the quotations" (*Mémoires*, 64).

I must quote but also interrupt the quotations. In the introduction to *Chaque fois unique*, Brault and Naas say that, in a first moment, quoting "without interruption" seems to be a way of avoiding indecency. As they then proceed to move beyond that "first moment," while they do not explicitly reference this statement Derrida made in *Memoires for Paul de Man*, they use a very similar formulation: "And so Derrida cites and interrupts the citation" (47, 24).[25]

If quoting without interruption seems, in a first moment, to be a way of avoiding indecency, is quoting *with* interruption a better way of avoiding indecency or is it instead an ethic of indecency? In the 1984 text on de Man where Derrida announces his double law, there is no mention of indecency; instead we find another ethically marked term, one more obviously connected to quotation: "At the limit of *fidelity* . . . a discourse 'in memory of' . . . could be content to quote. . . . Out of *fidelity*, one ought to quote . . . but one should not . . . be content to quote" (*Mémoires*, 64, emphasis added).

As Brault's and Naas's introduction progresses from saying that quoting without interruption seems to be a way of avoiding indecency to asserting that what Derrida in fact does is quote and interrupt, they too make reference to fidelity—or rather infidelity. They get the term "infidelity" from a paragraph in the memorial to Barthes. Quoting this paragraph at length, Brault and Naas treat it as another formulation of what Derrida says about the "double injunction" in the Lyotard essay. I concur and would like to quote this same paragraph at length here:

> Two infidelities, an impossible choice: on the one hand, say nothing . . . being content to quote, let him speak, efface one-self. . . . But this excess of fidelity would end up saying nothing, and exchanging nothing. . . . It . . . sends death back to death. On the other hand, by avoiding all quotation . . . so that what is addressed to Roland Barthes or speaks of him truly comes from the other, from the living friend, one risks making him disappear again, as if one could add death to death, and thus indecently pluralize it. (71–72, 45)

As Derrida sees it, the choice is not between fidelity and infidelity, but only between two opposing infidelities. Either we quote and thus silence our own voice, or we speak without quoting and relegate the other to silence. What is lost in either case is the "exchange," the possibility of two voices speaking to each other. The ethics of quotation would seem to be an ethics of dialogue.[26]

"Avoiding all quotation," we reduce the dead friend to silence, which risks killing him yet again. Indecency makes an appearance here, on this side of the equation, on the side of not quoting. If "avoiding quotation" can lead to indecency, then we might indeed think that quotation is a way to avoid indecency. (Brault and Naas: "Citation seems to avoid the indecency of speaking simply *of* the dead.") Here in this passage what is indecent is "pluralizing" death, adding insult to injury, death to death.[27] *And yet . . .* If Derrida finds pluralizing death indecent, then we must recall that the title of this piece is "The Death*s* of Roland Barthes" (a fact that he reminds us of at the end of this same paragraph).

With this essay in honor of Barthes, Derrida is, you will recall, writing for the first time in a genre he vowed never to write. As he articulates it in 1981, this genre involves breaking a promise to himself, a promise made, he explains parenthetically, out of concern for what we might want to call "fidelity" (77, 49). Appearing a few pages earlier in the same essay, the paragraph on two infidelities is his articulation of the ethical perils of the genre.

He takes up this genre again, for the second time, three years later, upon the death of his friend Paul de Man. And we can see a number of similarities between the "double law" passage from the memorial on de Man and this "double infidelity" paragraph from the Barthes essay. There is, as in so many of these memorial texts, the idea of letting the dead friend speak. But these two early texts in the genre specifically share both the phrase *se contenter de citer* (the idea of being content to quote, of limiting oneself to quoting) and the question of fidelity. In the 1984 lecture on de Man, being content to quote is "at the limit of fidelity"; in the 1981 essay on Barthes, being content to quote displays an "excess of fidelity." Although the paragraph quoted at length above opens with the symmetrical "two infidelities," what we find as the paragraph unfolds is that one of the infidelities is an "excess of fidelity."

On the very last page of his memorial to Barthes, Derrida tells us he is looking through, "almost at random," the book *Roland Barthes par Roland Barthes* and (in a parenthesis) he confesses: "I try to understand how he could write '*I don't like . . .* fidelity'" (97, 67, ellipsis Derrida's). Struggling to be faithful to Barthes, Derrida discovers, much to his confusion ("I try to understand how he could"), a passage where Barthes says he does not like fidelity. How to be faithful to someone who does not like fidelity?[28]

Trying to understand this surprising opinion, Derrida speculates, "I suppose . . . that in this case he didn't like a certain pathos that fidelity easily takes on, and above all the word, the discourse on fidelity the second it gets tired, becomes drab, lukewarm, faded, forbidding, unfaithful (*infidèle*)" (97, 67). Whatever Barthes might have meant by saying he does not like fidelity, Derrida connects it to the place where fidelity reaches a limit, an excess ("gets tired"), and becomes infidelity.

In the phrase "the second it gets tired, becomes lukewarm, faded," we might connect "the second" here to Derrida's frequent use of "the moment"; we might note that getting tired, becoming lukewarm, fading, are all processes that happen over time, processes in which something loses sharpness, heat, vividness as time goes by. In trying to understand Barthes's dislike for fidelity, Derrida envisions it in a temporal dimension. Fidelity, of course, is all about temporality; fidelity is a promise to remain constant, unchanging over time; it is a promise to resist temporality.

Quotation might seem to be a way of avoiding infidelity, in a first moment, but limiting oneself to quotation, at the limit of fidelity, one ends up committing another infidelity. *Two infidelities, an impossible choice.* "Derrida attempts to negotiate the passage between these two infidelities," according to Brault and Naas, "by citing the other, by recalling the other's words and then cutting them off" (47, 24). "Recalling the other's words" makes quotation sound respectful; "cutting them off" makes graphic the violence of interruption. Yet both represent poles of opposing, and inevitable, infidelities. Derrida attempts to negotiate the passage between the infidelity of violence and the infidelity of reverence.

What I have, in this chapter, been calling an ethics of indecency might also be called an ethics of infidelity. Although I chose indecency because of the striking prevalence of that term in *Chaque fois unique*, "infidelity" might have helped us see the way this ethics inhabits temporality.

:: :: ::

An early draft of the present chapter bore the title "Indecent, And Yet." This previous title reflected my desire to foreground how in these memorial essays Derrida articulated his ethical stance around the "and yet." I first saw this "and yet" in his foreword to *Chaque fois unique*, and I kept coming upon it as I read the collection—sometimes in that same exact phrase, sometimes in other phrases like "but nonetheless." I found it also in the 1984 memorial for de Man which, while not included in the collection, articulates the ethical imperative of the genre, in the form of a double law: "One ought to quote in the desire to let the other speak *but* one should not . . . be content to quote. It is with the law of this double law that we are here engaged. . . . I thus must quote *but also* interrupt the quotations" (*Mémoires*, 64, emphasis added). The double law is articulated around the conjunction "but." The "but" here, and the "but also," are akin to "and yet"—share in the ethics of, and the logic of, the "and yet."

While "and yet" is no longer in the title of the present chapter, the title of our previous chapter still sports a "but." I think the logic of Derrida's "and yet" is very close to what in reading Barthes I called perverse logic. Barthes knows the author is dead *but* nonetheless desires him; Derrida feels that these memorials to his dead friends are indecent *and yet* he writes and publishes them just the same. Barthes's perversity and Derrida's indecency are both, I would say, responses to the author's death. These responses share a contrary logic; in Barthes that logic leans toward the erotic while Derrida's contradictory logic stands in the ethical.

The previous chapter connected, if ever so lightly, Barthes's perverse logic with gay sexuality; in this chapter the indecency has to do with friendship—we read Derrida's loving response to his friends, all male friends (with one exception). Where Barthes's response to the author's death involves desire and bodies, Derrida's response is more personal. In my attempt to make the "death of the author" refer not only to the literary theoretical concept but also to real loss, I proceed from Barthes to Derrida. While our reading of Barthes adds poignancy and desire to what had become an overly familiar catchphrase, the author's death remains nonetheless a theoretical death. As we move to Derrida—whose response to the death of the author literally begins in response to Barthes's actual death—we encounter a more personal relation to the author's death, a reader's mourning for a dear, departed author. I find in Derrida's memorial essays, and in particular in his memorial for Barthes, not just personal mourning, but a composite of the personal sense of loss with a more general theory of the author. While Derrida feels this mix of mourning and theory to be itself indecent, I prize it as a powerful reconceptualization of the "death of the author."

::

PART II

::

If I Were a Writer and Dead

OUR FIRST CHAPTER devoted a long, slow reading to one paragraph, the penultimate paragraph from the preface to *Sade, Fourier, Loyola.* This mother lode of a paragraph allowed us a fuller, richer understanding of Barthes's conceptualization of the author, far beyond the familiar, one-dimensional slogan. The paragraph begins by announcing "a friendly return of the author," returning from the death Barthes proclaimed just three years earlier. Lingering on many of its evocative words and phrases, my reading of the paragraph culminates, ultimately stops on the strange and wondrous fantasy: "If I were a writer, and dead, how I would love it if my life . . . could . . . come to touch . . . some future body. . . ."[1] I revisit this paragraph now in order to emphasize what the first chapter only remarked in passing: that as Barthes thinks the return of the dead author, he shifts (within the same paragraph) from the perspective of the reader ("the author . . . comes from his text and goes into our life") to that of the writer ("if I were a writer, and dead . . . how I would love it"). As if to really think through his relation to the author, to think through the erotics of the reader/author relation, to move beyond the flat and lifeless polemic against the author, Barthes must pass from the reader's standpoint to speaking as a writer (if only in fantasy).

The present book will follow Barthes in this move. While part I opened up the death of the author to a wider range of meanings, its two chapters remained within the reader's perspective. Part II will shift to consider the death of the author from the point of view of the writer. The following two chapters will reflect on how the death of the author looks to the writer, how the author's death haunts the writer writing.

Chapter 3

THE QUEER TEMPORALITY OF WRITING

::

In the last chapter, we looked at how Derrida negotiates a persistent sense of indecency in and about writing memorials for his friends. Perhaps the most indecent thing for Derrida is the recognition that these mourning essays constitute a genre. If all these heartfelt acts of mourning belong to a genre, then the poignancy seems conventional rather than authentic. The generic nature of these memorials was foregrounded when they were collected together and published as a book; reading this collection, the previous chapter focused on the generic, on issues posed by this genre.

The present chapter continues our exploration of this ethically problematic and theoretically invaluable genre. We turn here to two memorial essays by Eve Kosofsky Sedgwick. Written in 1990 and 1991, Sedgwick's memorials not only date from the same period as those in Derrida's collection,[1] but they belong very much to the same genre. Her memorials are both written on the occasion of the death of a friend; both friends are also authors Sedgwick has read; both memorials combine personal mourning with intellectual work.

Sedgwick's memorials are both included in *Tendencies*, a 1993 collection of her essays. While we found Derrida's mourning pieces in a collection devoted exclusively to the genre, we find Sedgwick's memorials alongside essays devoted to long dead authors like Oscar Wilde and Henry James. While *Chaque fois unique* resists treating recently deceased friends like other authors that Derrida writes about, *Tendencies* makes us see the memorials as part of her larger critical work. In this chapter, we will read Sedgwick's memorial essays in the context of this 1993 volume.

Sedgwick is widely recognized as one of the founders and leading lights of queer theory, and *Tendencies* is in fact the book where she foregrounds the idea of "queer." Reading her two mourning essays in this book helps us read them as part of queer theory. The essays are in honor of Craig Owens and Michael Lynch, both gay writers who died of AIDS, and the incorporation of their memorials in her work bespeaks the general way that mourning became a central part of queer theory. While for Derrida the connection between mourning and theoretical insight seemed unjustifiable and indecent, for Sedgwick, writing in the ethical context of the queer response to AIDS, this connection looks quite different. Queer theory in the early nineties was energized—and politically justified—by the embrace of precisely such indecencies.

Writing about dead authors, friends recently dead of AIDS, Sedgwick displays both the perverse desire Barthes theorizes in my first chapter and the ethics of indecency Derrida proffers in my second. If for Derrida the indecency was located in the memorial genre, in Sedgwick's mourning essays what is indecent has more to do with the moment, with timing.[2] Sedgwick's memorial writing, as we read it in *Tendencies*, is the site of an indecent, perverse, uncanny encounter with temporality.

∷ ∷ ∷

The opening to *Tendencies* is all about time. The foreword—entitled "T Times"—begins by discussing T-shirts seen at the 1992 gay pride parade in New York; surveying the T's, Sedgwick concludes, "It was a QUEER time."[3] Echoing this declaration, the next paragraph states: "I suppose this must be called the moment of Queer" (xii). More emphatically than anywhere else in her oeuvre, here in the opening to *Tendencies* Sedgwick announces "Queer," loudly proclaims "QUEER." This proclamation of queer is, it would seem, insistently temporal—a queer *time*, the *moment* of queer.

In an essay published in 2002, Stephen Barber and David Clark focus on this very temporal dimension of Sedgwick's queer. Closely reading Sedgwick's proclamation, Barber and Clark remark the peculiarity of what she actually says: "Even the ingenuously jubilant claim . . . 'It was a QUEER time,' comes to us by way of the past tense, and for all the mounted evidence *for* the queer moment offered in surrounding sentences, conclusive conviction is hedged by a prefatory supposition: 'I suppose this must be called the moment of Queer.'"[4] *Jubilant but hedging*: Barber and Clark make us see just what an odd speech act Sedgwick's proclamation in fact is.

Barber and Clark go on to propose a way to understand such peculiarity: "Sedgwick's reluctance in 1993 to affirm decisively that this *is* the queer moment . . . suggests that a problem about temporality may be for her a defining aspect of that moment. Sedgwick . . . initially seems to cast the span of 'queer' within a recognizably temporal frame, but what remains evident in the [foreword] to *Tendencies*, as across the entire body of her work, is another conception and unfolding of temporality, a specifically queer temporality."

I concur. I share Barber's and Clark's sense of Sedgwick's "problem about temporality"; I subscribe to their idea that "another conception and unfolding of temporality" is evident in Sedgwick's work. I would underline that this other temporality is "a defining aspect of that moment" which Sedgwick calls (however ambiguously) queer—the moment around 1992 that produces not only the foreword to *Tendencies* but also the two memorial essays included in the 1993 book.

The present chapter should be seen as an elaboration of what Barber and Clark call Sedgwick's "queer temporality." Barber and

Clark may be the first to use this phrase, which has since come to name a major trend within queer theory.[5] Their reading of Sedgwick is certainly one of the earliest examples of this trend. Where Barber and Clark derive Sedgwick's queer temporality from the foreword to *Tendencies*, we will look at how this temporality plays out in and around her memorial writing in the same volume.

Barber's and Clark's formulation of Sedgwick's temporality takes as its epigraph some lines from a poem by Sedgwick. The lines include the evocative phrase "this rack of temporalities." Although they never comment directly on the epigraph, a few pages later, Barber and Clark parenthetically allude to this particular phrase, saying that Sedgwick's queer moment is "defined . . . by the twists it gives (on that 'rack') to all other temporalities" (4). These "twists" suggest another name for queer temporality; twisted is a good name for the temporality I find in Sedgwick's memorials.

The "rack of temporalities" comes from a poem Sedgwick published in 1994, just a year after *Tendencies*. Here is part of the poem's first stanza, which instantiates her reference (in the second stanza) to "this rack of temporalities": "Guys who were 35 last year are 70 this year / . . . / A killing velocity—seen another way, though, / they've ambled onto the eerily slow-mo / extermination camp the city sidewalks are."[6] While the "rack" here clearly connotes a scene of torture, the primary meaning of "this rack" has to do with the twisting of temporality. A year is not a year: "guys" can age 35 years in one year. Such "velocity" is already a distortion but Sedgwick then gives it another twist: this "killing velocity—seen another way" can be "eerily slow-mo." Temporality here is so tortuous that terrifying speed can be, at the same time, hauntingly slow.

This is a poem about AIDS. In Sedgwick's 1994 collection of poetry, this poem appears in a group of nine poems about gay men dying of AIDS. At least one of the poems is about Michael Lynch, subject of one of the memorials in *Tendencies*. While a couple of these poems are about the generality of gay men dying young, all the beloved individuals dying in these poems, all the dying friends, are writers. One of the poems ends: "a writer, just turned 32."[7]

The first poem about a dying gay writer opens: "No good outcomes with this disease/ but good days, yes—that's the unit/ for now, the day: good day, bad day."[8] The last of this group of poems begins, "It is the long moment of no more/ Goodbye in our vocabulary."[9] Moments, days, years: Sedgwick's poems about gay-men-dying-with-AIDS have an insistent temporal dimension. The particular poem that Barber and Clark take as their epigraph not only alludes to that dimension but theorizes it, calling AIDS "this rack of temporalities." Beginning by quoting this poem, Barber and Clark want us to see that Sedgwick's queer temporality is bound up with AIDS. Again, I concur.

AIDS is also present in the declaration of the queer moment that opens *Tendencies*. If that declaration is jubilant but hedging, AIDS is part of the hedge: "I suppose this must be called the moment of Queer. *(Though it's other moments, too. . . . Long moment of a deathly silence that means the AIDS drugs we've been struggling to hold on for are just not in the pipeline. When Melvin Dixon and Tom Yingling disappear from us. . . .)*" (xii).

The parenthesis actually begins with a sentence fragment, with what grammatically belongs to the sentence announcing the queer moment: "I suppose this must be called the moment of Queer, though it's other moments, too." The parenthesis then goes on for five sentences to catalog various aspects of gay politics at the beginning of 1993.[10] In the list of current gay political issues, included as alternative ways to characterize this moment—in the long parenthesis in italics included as an alternative to the main text—we find AIDS, and death.[11]

While Sedgwick's queer time is bound up with AIDS, I want to note the tension between the two in this passage. Where her announcement of "a QUEER time" may be jubilant, AIDS is part of a hedging afterthought. Far from integrated into the text, it is italicized and parenthesized, represented as what can be neither integrated nor forgotten. AIDS is, for sure, part of *Tendencies*'s queer temporality, but it is not an easy part, does not fit comfortably.

The long parenthesis distorts the text, twists it out of shape. AIDS and death are part of that distortion.

The long italicized parenthesis, having brought up AIDS and "deathly silence," goes on to name Melvin Dixon and Tom Yingling. Dixon was a playwright, Yingling an academic literary critic; both writers were gay men who died of AIDS in 1992. Although these two dead authors are never again mentioned in *Tendencies*, never appear outside the parenthesis, the book does include memorials for two other gay writers who died of AIDS. It is as if the memorial essays bore some relation to the italicized parenthesis, to the neither-integrated-nor-forgotten "other moments" that haunt Sedgwick's announcement of a queer time.

Bearing Barber and Clark's reading of Sedgwick's queer temporality in mind, I want now to look closely at the two memorial pieces in *Tendencies*. Written during the period Sedgwick calls the queer moment, the two memorials—separately but especially together—turn out to be rich sites of twisting and twisted temporality. While the time-twisting involves, as you might expect, death, it also, more surprisingly, involves writing.

:: :: ::

In the middle of *Tendencies* we find a three-paragraph text entitled "Memorial for Craig Owens." Owens was an art critic, not a particularly close friend of Sedgwick's, more of a casual acquaintance. He died of AIDS-related illness in 1990; a month after his death Sedgwick delivered a short piece at a memorial in New York. The memorial's first paragraph characterizes their relationship. It opens with a short and somewhat mysterious sentence: "Craig's and my relation was fragmentary and public." The second sentence elaborates: "this fairly strange . . . form of love, the love of part-objects, snatches of print, glimpses and touches of a largely unfamiliar body." "Part-objects," "snatches," "glimpses and touches": these begin to explain her declaration that their relation is "fragmentary."

Sedgwick's "fragmentary" recalls Roland Barthes's preference for the "fragment" (a preference explored in our first chapter). In fact, while the occasion and genre of this little memorial takes us back to Derrida's relation to the author friend, Sedgwick describes her relationship to Owens in terms very similar to what we saw in Barthes's erotic relation to the author.[12]

"Part-objects" is a Freudian term; "the love of part-objects" is a quasi-Freudian way of designating perverse sexuality.[13] While Freud's use of "part-objects" might imply the inferiority of such perverse, fragmentary love (inferior to some mature love of the whole person), Sedgwick's redeployment of it renders her "fragmentary" relation to Owens a mode of queer sexuality. In the context of queer theory, to characterize a "form of love" as "fairly strange" is, of course, more likely to celebrate than to disqualify it.

While Sedgwick stresses the erotic and bodily nature of their relation—"glimpses and touches of a largely unfamiliar body"—this bodily relation involves "snatches of print." It may be a perverse sexual relation, but the part-objects are pieces of published writing, which begins to explain what she means by her declaration that their relation is "fragmentary and public."

Sedgwick ends the first paragraph of her memorial to Owens with a final depiction of their relation: "this strange, utterly discontinuous, projective space of desire, euphemistically named friendship, love at a distance, or even just reading and writing" (105). Once again she characterizes their relation as "strange" (and again I hear that word's synonymy with "queer"). This sort of relation is usually named "friendship," but Sedgwick sees that as a "euphemism," denying the perverse "desire" that is part of her portrait.[14] Rejecting the name "friendship" (while admitting that is what it is likely to be called), she again uses the term "love," and then adds her ultimate name: "reading and writing."

This placement of reading and writing in the framework of perverse sexuality has much in common with Barthes's celebration of the perverse reader in *The Pleasure of the Text*. "The pleasure of the Text also includes," according to Barthes, "a friendly return of the author."[15] Despite her suspicion that the term is a euphemism, the sort of "friendship" Sedgwick is talking about here could well be a version of Barthes's friendly return of the author. In recounting her relationship to Owens, Sedgwick tells a tale of queer desire, but the desire occurs in a relation of reading and writing. "Craig entered my life in the most seductive of guises: in print . . . he didn't send this essay of his to me; I found it in a book in a bookstore" (104). Sedgwick reads an essay, and its author "enter[s her] life." In this idea of the author entering her life, we again hear echoes of Barthes's relation to the author: "The author who comes from his text and goes into our life . . . is a body."[16]

Notwithstanding Sedgwick's use of words like "love" and "desire," and phrases like "touches of a body," her relation to Owens is in fact a relation of reading and writing: the relationship starts when Sedgwick reads an essay. Owens did not send Sedgwick the essay; she found it in a bookstore; their relation is "public." As he enters Sedgwick's life, Owens is not just a writer but indeed an author.

The essay Sedgwick finds in a bookstore is Owens's 1987 "Outlaws: Gay Men in Feminism." Criticizing the generally homophobic relation to gay men in feminist writing, "Outlaws" singles out Sedgwick's 1985 book *Between Men* for praise. When Owens enters Sedgwick's life, he is not only an author, he is her reader. "He did me the incredible honor of finding my work usable" (104). His essay gives her a gratifying image of herself as an author.

In a preface to *Between Men*, Sedgwick tells us that during the writing of the book, she "actually knew only one openly gay man." This retrospective preface (written in 1992) goes on to say: "There's a way in which the author of this book seems not quite to have been able to believe in the reality of the gay male communities toward whose readership the book so palpably yearns."[17] In this text written just two years after the Owens memorial, Sedgwick speaks of her 1985 book's desire for readers. Referring to herself in the third person as "the author," she gestures toward a sort of Barthesian desire, not personal but textual, yet nonetheless "palpable," a desire reaching out, beyond the author's personal limitations, toward readers. The book Owens reads and praises is a book that "palpably yearns" for gay male readers like Owens; no wonder Sedgwick found him "seductive."

Owens's 1987 essay occasions his entry into Sedgwick's life, but its place in their relationship is more than just a beginning. In fact this same essay is still playing a central role in her relation to him at the moment he dies. Sedgwick actually speaks of the essay twice in her short memorial for Owens, but she does so in such a way that a reader would not know she is talking about the same text. She mentions it in the first paragraph, telling the story of how their relation began; it returns later in the "Memorial" as part of the account of her particular grief at his death.

The penultimate paragraph of the "Memorial" turns from describing their relationship to explaining Sedgwick's feelings about Owens's death. She separates her feelings into two parts—one quite general, the other quite peculiar. The first part of her grief bespeaks her pro-gay, AIDS politics; it is social and political. The first aspect of her grief is what she might feel about any gay man dying of AIDS. The "Memorial" devotes one sentence to this general, political aspect of her feelings; the rest of the "Memorial" then, a paragraph and a half, elaborates the second part.

The second aspect of her grief is, as she puts it, "more local." This second part is, as it turns out, all about reading and writing, and it also involves the text through which Owens entered her life: "Three weeks ago I was halfway through writing an essay whose intellectual motive came, as it happened, from a couple of cryptic paragraphs of Craig's" (105). At the moment he died she was coincidentally ("as it happened") writing an essay whose "intellectual motive" (i.e., source, influence, inspiration) came from "a couple of paragraphs of Craig's." The fact that she identifies her source not as the entire essay but as "a couple of paragraphs" fits her characterization of her relation to Owens as "fragmentary"—her "intellectual motive" appears in the form of what she calls "snatches of print." While the "Memorial" does not tell us where these "cryptic paragraphs" were found, elsewhere in *Tendencies* we learn that the paragraphs are from the same 1987 essay

("Outlaws") through whose seduction Owens entered her life.[18] This same essay of Owens is there at the beginning and, "as it happened," there again (or still) at the end of Sedgwick's relation to him.

At the moment he died, Sedgwick was writing an essay that had in fact a double relation to Owens: "an essay whose intellectual motive came . . . from a couple of cryptic paragraphs of Craig's . . . and whose writerly motive . . . came *entirely* from the fun of imagining sending it to him . . . invoking Craig's eyes to read it through" (105–6). Not only did Owens provide the "intellectual motive" of this essay, he also furnishes Sedgwick with what she calls her "writerly motive." If her "intellectual motive" involved "snatches of print," her writerly motive also involves what Sedgwick calls "part-objects," this motive more bodily— "Craig's eyes."

This strange projective space of desire named reading and writing: while Sedgwick's "intellectual motive" positions her as a reader of Owens, her "writerly motive" is a fantasy of the reverse relation—imagining him reading her. The fantasy motivating her writing is a sort of circle of reciprocal reading and writing. Or rather, since the Owens essay that provided her "intellectual motive" was originally his reading of Sedgwick, it would be more like a chain of reading and writing—him reading her reading him reading her. Yet whether the fantasy motivating her writing is circular or serial, Owens's death abruptly and absolutely interrupts it. "I was halfway through writing an essay . . . whose writerly motive . . . came . . . from . . . imagining sending it to him. . . . And then suddenly I couldn't do that." When Owens died, her "writerly motive" died.

Sedgwick's grief at Owens's death is completely bound up with an essay she was writing at the time. Moreover, she devotes fully half of her memorial for Owens to her feelings about the essay she was writing. What is perhaps most peculiar about this memorial, what Derrida might call most indecent, is that she mourns her loss as a writer.

Owens and Sedgwick had a relationship very much like those

memorialized in Derrida's *Work of Mourning*. For example, the final essay in that volume, "Lyotard and *Us*," has Derrida reading Lyotard reading Derrida. While *The Work of Mourning* explicitly categorizes those memorialized as "authors," most of them are also readers of Derrida. The memorials, however, treat them as authors rather than readers; Derrida mourns as a reader rather than a writer, as if that were the decent thing to do.

Owens enters Sedgwick's life as an author (found in a book in a bookstore), and that is his position at the beginning of her memorial. As "Memorial for Craig Owens" opens, we are not only in the same configuration we saw in Derrida's memorials, mourning the death of the author/friend, but also in the relation theorized by Barthes, where the author comes from his text and enters the reader's life. At the beginning of Sedgwick's memorial for Owens, we thus find ourselves in the territory traversed in our first two chapters, part I of the present book. But by the end of this memorial, as she focuses on her own writing, Owens becomes more reader than author. By the end of her memorial, Sedgwick is mourning not so much the loss of a beloved author, but something we might call the death of the reader, the death of her reader.

Let us now follow the path of Sedgwick's first memorial, moving from a readerly to a writerly perspective on death. Viewed from within the drama of writing, death takes on some particular resonances. Reading Sedgwick's account of her loss, I notice how insistent are the marks of temporality. While death is always necessarily about temporality, her particular story of losing Owens is all about the temporality of writing. While death is generally a reminder of the fragility of life, the story Sedgwick tells about her reaction to Owens's death is about the fragility of writing, a fragility that has everything to do with writing's temporal aspect.

Consider again her words: "Three weeks ago I was halfway through writing an essay whose intellectual motive came . . . from a couple of cryptic paragraphs of Craig's that I had been *worrying over for a long time*; and whose writerly motive, when the essay turned out to be much harder to think through and enjoy than I'd expected, came . . . from . . . imagining sending it to him if I could ever finish it. . . . *And then suddenly* I couldn't do that" (105–6, emphasis added). This story unfolds in a markedly temporal dimension; it is in fact the account of a clash between two different temporal modalities — the slow modality of "worrying over for a long time" runs up against the abrupt instantaneous modality of "And then suddenly."

In her memorial for Owens, Sedgwick talks about what a hard time she is having writing. Even before she started writing the essay, she had been, as she puts it, "worrying over" Owens's "cryptic" paragraphs "for a long time," suggesting not only that they had stuck in her mind but that she was having trouble figuring them out. And then, after this long time of "worrying" that preceded the writing, "the essay turned out to be much harder to think through and to enjoy than [she]'d expected."

Sedgwick underscores how difficult writing was, and especially how crucial her fantasy of Owens reading it was to keeping her going: "whose writerly motive . . . came *entirely* from the fun of imagining sending it to him." Sedgwick italicizes "entirely," emphasizing that there was nothing else to keep her going in this surprisingly difficult writing. And even with the help of her fantasy of being read by Owens, the fate of the writing remained seriously in doubt: "imagining sending it to him *if I could ever finish it*" (emphasis added).

This passage contains yet a third temporal modality, one even more bound up with writing. When Sedgwick claims she is "halfway through," while it may refer to how many pages she has written or how much of her topic she has covered, it is also a temporal claim, alluding to some future in which the essay would be finished. This third temporal modality is a relation to futurity — a relation I see most directly in Sedgwick's "imagining sending it to him if I could ever finish it." While not strictly speaking a future tense, "if I could ever finish" is what grammarians call a conditional. This verb form is probably the most authentic modality to talk about the future, given a constitutive uncertainty about what the future holds. Though death is of course one of the principal names of this insecurity about the future, the anxiety that can so easily accompany writing is also always grappling with the conditionality of that future completion that might not come.[19]

The conditional relation to futurity is all about expectations and surprises, about the gap between expectations and how things "turn out." This gap will be the major theme of Sedgwick's memorial for Michael Lynch, written less than a year after her memorial for Owens. We will turn to the Lynch memorial in the next section of this chapter, pursuing further this third temporal modality and elaborating how this jarring discrepancy plays out in Sedgwick's writing practice.

In the Owens memorial, we can hear this gap between expectation and outcome quietly at work when Sedgwick says, "The essay turned out to be much harder to think through and to enjoy than I expected." While the big surprise in Sedgwick's account is, to be sure, Owens's death, I cannot help but notice that this surprise functions as a repetition of a prior surprise, which is how "much harder" the essay was to write than she had "expected."

I cannot help but notice that in this memorial, death intervenes as a repetition of Sedgwick's difficulty writing. I find this repetition unsettling. I must confess to being a bit shocked that "Memorial for Craig Owens" talks at length and in detail about what a hard time Sedgwick has been having writing. I must also confess to finding this focus on writing in the context of death theoretically rich. Thinking through death from within her writing practice, Sedgwick brings to light the haunted temporality of writing. This temporality, with its theoretical riches and memorial indecencies, is repeated and exacerbated in the "obituary" she writes the following year for Michael Lynch.

:: :: ::

While the reader of the Owens memorial is left with a poignant sense of the impossibility of Sedgwick's finishing the essay she was writing at the time, it turns out that the memorial's sense of impossibility is in fact only momentary. *Tendencies* actually includes a completed version of the very essay Sedgwick was half-way through writing when Owens died. This quite wonderful essay appears earlier in the same section of the book as "Memorial for Craig Owens."[20] The essay's endnote covers some of the same ground as the "Memorial," telling us that it "was sparked by the work of Craig Owens" and that "any pleasure in its writing came from the anticipation of showing it to him," concluding: "That was the least of the things that suddenly became impossible on his death from AIDS-related illness, on 4 July 1990" (72). While the endnote thus echoes the memorial's sense of sudden impossibility, it puts Sedgwick's peculiar, writerly grief in perspective ("*the least of the things* that suddenly became impossible"). Owens's death is here no longer linked to the fragility of Sedgwick's writing; indeed the endnote tells us that the essay "was written in the summer of 1990"—the essay that in July looked impossible to finish seems to have been completed only a month or two after the Memorial.

This 1990 essay is entitled "Tales of the Avunculate"; Sedgwick gets the term "avunculate" (meaning the relation between maternal uncle and nephew) from those "cryptic paragraphs" of Owens.[21] Following Owens, Sedgwick expands the term out from its anthropological meaning to cover all sorts of uncles and aunts (often the locus of the queer in the family), and—through an uncle-centered reading of Wilde's *Importance of Being Earnest*— she offers the avunculate as a queer alternative to the normative family.

After twenty pages of brilliant, playful exploration of the queerness of uncles, however, Sedgwick's completed essay ultimately ends by going beyond the avunculate. In a surprising move, the final paragraph abruptly turns away from the celebration of uncles, and "Tales of the Avunculate" ends with a militant rejection of the family. This last paragraph begins by quoting a critique of the family made in December 1989 by "one gay scholar/activist, Michael Lynch" (71). If Owens gets credit for this essay's origin, Lynch, it would seem, presides over its ending. Lynch, it would seem, authorizes Sedgwick to move beyond Owens, allowing Sedgwick to finish.[22]

That the 1990 essay whose writing was endangered by Owens's death should end by turning to Michael Lynch seems more than ironic. Although Lynch is alive when Sedgwick completes "Tales of the Avunculate" in the summer of 1990, he will himself die of AIDS a year later. Lynch will become the subject of the second memorial piece in *Tendencies*, "White Glasses," the extraordinary essay that closes the volume.

The two memorial texts are theoretically congruent. The 1990 memorial uses the Freudian notion of the part-object in order to inscribe Sedgwick's relation to Owens under the sign of perverse sexuality. The memorial for Lynch helps us theorize just this sort of insistence on perverse sexuality in our mourning, via a quotation from Michael Moon: "I am arguing . . . for the desirability, indeed, the necessity . . . of allowing our sex radicalism to pervade our mourning practices. . . . We want to conduct our mourning and grieving in the image of, and as an indispensable part of, this task of . . . exploring 'perverse' or stigmatized desire."[23]

Theoretically then, Sedgwick's memorials take us back to my inquiry in part I, combining Barthes's explicitly perverse desire for the dead with Derrida's mourning and grieving. In the texts we read in our first two chapters, Barthes could desire the dead but only abstractly and thus without grief; Derrida, on the other hand, could grieve his loss but only while feeling abashed by his own indecency. The context of queer theory in the early 1990s — trying to affirm perverse, stigmatized desire in the face of AIDS and death — made it not only possible but crucial to articulate at one and the same time both desire and loss, both radical perversity and grief. The theoretical advance produced in the present book by bringing Derrida's mourning pieces into conjunction with Barthes's desire for the dead author is, I would say, already operative in Sedgwick's queer memorials.

Quoting Michael Moon, the Lynch memorial supplies a theory to explain Sedgwick's insistence on part-objects in her earlier memorial. While both memorials cite a number of part-objects in portraying Sedgwick's desiring relation to the deceased friend, it is a particular part-object that serves as the most striking connection between the two mourning texts. In 1990, Sedgwick tells us that "the only pleasure" she felt about her writing came in "invoking Craig's eyes to read it through" (106). A year later she writes: "So often I feel that I see with Michael's eyes" (257).

In the memorial to Owens, "Craig's eyes" connect both to perverse sexuality and to reading and writing, to the nexus that makes the reader/writer relation a queer bodily encounter. In 1991, "Michael's eyes" are part of the dominant frame that gives the memorial its title. "White Glasses" opens with Sedgwick's account of how, upon seeing Lynch for the first time, she instantly resolved that she must have a pair of white-framed glasses like those he was wearing. While it took her quite some time to find them, during the last few years of his life Sedgwick wore glasses like his, which surely must be connected to this feeling that she "sees with Michael's eyes."

On the dedication page to *Tendencies*, under a dedication to Lynch, we see photographs of Lynch and Sedgwick together in a graveyard, both wearing their white glasses. Photographs of the two in their matching glasses appear again at the other end of the volume, this time textually. The entirety of section 8 of "White Glasses" is a long quotation from a letter to Sedgwick's brother, a quotation that opens: "If you leafed through the enclosed snapshots before getting to the prose, you'll have inferred from the unusual prevalence of *white enameled glasses* that we had . . . a . . . visit from my Toronto friend Michael" (258). Enclosing snapshots that the reader will look at "before getting to the prose" is in fact a gesture Sedgwick repeats in the book *Tendencies* by including snapshots on the dedication page, snapshots like the ones she sent her brother, maybe even the very same ones.

While I find Sedgwick's quoting from a letter to her brother touching and I relish the wit of her phrase "the unusual prevalence of *white enameled glasses*" (emphasis in the original), what really grabs me about this quotation from her letter is a problem with its temporality. Section 8 of "White Glasses" opens: "From a letter to my little brother in the summer of 1987" (258). Four pages earlier, section 3 opens: "It took me a year and a half . . . to find glasses that I thought looked like Michael's" (254). Section 1 tells us repeatedly that Sedgwick first saw Lynch and his white glasses in December 1986. If it took her "a year and a half" after December 1986 to find a pair of white glasses for herself, then she could *not* have been wearing white glasses "in the summer of 1987."

I'm sure my concern seems petty. It hardly matters to her point about "white glasses," about her relation to Michael Lynch, that these dates don't line up. And yet every time I read "White Glasses," I find myself stuck on this dating, doing the calculations, and bothered by the discrepancy.

Sedgwick does make a point of these dates; they are in the text, not the notes. Although the dating of the letter to her brother or even of finding her white frames may be trivial, there is no question that "White Glasses" is a text very much marked by dates, a text that insists upon dates, beginning with it telling us repeatedly the date when Sedgwick first met Lynch. "White Glasses" is in fact a text where there is something peculiar going on with dates—a text where we run into dates that fail to line up as expected.

"White Glasses" was originally presented at a conference at the CUNY Center for Lesbian and Gay Studies, on May 9, 1991. Although it is a memorial piece, written for her dear friend, it was written for this occasion. Sedgwick tells us that, four months earlier, she "decided to write 'White Glasses' for this conference" (254). This is the familiar temporality of such academic occasional pieces: we must think in advance of a topic in relation to an occasion and then write for that deadline.

Sedgwick actually tells us twice about the moment of choosing this topic, both times in prominent locations in the text. Section 2 opens: "Four months ago when I decided to write 'White Glasses' for this conference I thought it was going to be an obituary for Michael Lynch" (254). Section 4 opens: "When I decided to write 'White Glasses' four months ago, I thought my friend Michael Lynch was dying" (255). While the temporality of an academic conference paper may be familiar, in the case of this paper what transpired between the moment of choosing a topic and the occasion for delivering the paper was completely unexpected.

In January 1991, Lynch's death seems "imminent" (254), and so Sedgwick decides that at the May conference she will present an obituary for him. But "within the space of a couple weeks, we were dealing with a breathtaking revival of Michael's energy" (255). When she speaks at the conference, on May 9, 1991, Lynch is still alive.

"When I decided to write 'White Glasses' four months ago, I thought my friend Michael Lynch was dying. . . . I thought I knew back then that assigning myself this task in advance . . . was a good way to deal prospectively and perhaps lucidly with a process of shock and mourning" (255–56).

"When I decided . . . I thought. . . . I thought I knew back then": this is the temporality of irony or maybe the irony of temporality. The irony is at the expense of Sedgwick's past self. The contrast is between past certainty—"I decided," "I thought I knew"—and present perspective, which makes a mockery of that past certainty. Past knowledge is revealed as naïveté. "Four months ago" becomes "back then"; "four months" turns out to be the yawning gap between confident knowledge and foolish presumption.

What Sedgwick thought she "knew back then" was itself of a temporal nature. She imagined it was a good idea to "assign [herself] this task *in advance*"; she figured it would be good "to deal *prospectively* with a process of shock and mourning." Such an idea could hardly help but be presumptuous. ("Presume" itself is etymologically temporal: from Latin, "to take in advance," from *prae-*, before.) How can we "deal prospectively" with "shock"? Doesn't "shock" necessarily involve surprise, unpreparedness? (Shock: "something that jars the mind or emotions as if with a violent, *unexpected* blow.")[24]

In the summer of 1990, Sedgwick is writing an essay she wants Craig Owens to read. She is taken by surprise when Owens dies before she finishes writing it. Less than a year later, Sedgwick is writing a conference presentation presuming Michael Lynch will be dead by the time she finishes. Contrary to her expectations, he is still alive when she presents the paper at the conference.

In looking at the memorial for Owens, I remarked on the clash of temporalities, how the temporality of sudden shock cut short the unfolding of Sedgwick's writing process, how death interrupted her writing pleasure. Looking at the temporal dimension of her plan for the Lynch memorial, it seems as if she were trying to avoid that sort of shock, trying to prepare for death, to make her writing sync up with death. And yet once again, despite her preparation, she is taken by surprise.

While the relations between writing and death would seem in these two cases to be diametrically opposed (surprised by death versus surprised by no death), they nonetheless also seem like a repetition. What is repeated is unexpectedness. It's as if her very presumption to prepare for "shock and mourning" were tempting fate to come surprise her from behind, from the direction opposite to how she was facing.[25]

Reading together these two memorials for gay men who died of AIDS, we can see the death that came too late (after she was finished writing) as a repetition of the death that came too soon (before she was finished writing). Seeing the two not as opposites but as somehow the same, we enter a temporal twist not unlike what we saw in Sedgwick's poem where men with AIDS were both aging too fast and also moving too slow.

As an obituary for someone who is still alive, "White Glasses" is just extremely troubling and perverse; its indecency is not in what it says, but in its temporality. Read together with the Owens memorial, the obituary's already quite queer temporality becomes even more twisted.

:: :: ::

"When I decided to write 'White Glasses' four months ago, *I thought* my friend Michael Lynch was dying. . . . *I thought* I knew back then that assigning myself this task in advance . . . *I thought* it was a good way to deal prospectively . . . with a process of . . . mourning. . . . *I thought* I would have to—*I thought* I could—address this to you instead of to Michael; and now (yikes) I can do both" (255–56, emphasis added). *I thought, I thought, I thought, I thought.* The repetition of this phrase makes it sound like a criticism of thinking, a self-criticism of someone who thinks too much; Sedgwick's past naïveté would seem to be a form of intellectualism. The irony directed at Sedgwick's past self is unrelenting.

The last sentence quoted here, however, takes us beyond self-irony. Addressing her conference audience directly ("you"), she explains that the paper turned out to have a double address (Michael and you).[26] The tone is upbeat—"I thought I would have to . . . and now I can"—as Sedgwick seems to move from sad necessity to happy possibility.[27] The parenthesis in the sentence—"(yikes)"—is the most direct expression of emotion in the entire paper. A quick search online tells me this is an interjection used to express "mild fear or surprise."[28] While the tone is undoubtedly playful ("mild"), I would say that Sedgwick is here expressing both surprise and fear. My reading so far has been focused on surprise, which I see as part of the temporality of the ironic twist. Surprise and fear have different temporal orientations: while surprise has to do with the gap between past and present, fear is a relation to futurity.

Sedgwick herself links fear to temporality: "I thought I would have to . . . address this to you instead of to Michael; and now (yikes) I can do both. The I who does both is also a different one with new fears and temporalities" (256). This is the only appearance in "White Glasses" of the word "temporality"—the only appearance of the word Barber and Clark have made so central to their reading of Sedgwick, the word we use in the title to the present chapter.[29] Sedgwick's temporalities are here coupled with fears, and both are connected to the fact that, not only is her addressee different than what she expected when she decided to write "White Glasses," but so is the speaker, so is she. Yikes, indeed!

While quoting the self-ironic passage from section 4, I have,

I must confess, intentionally and repeatedly left out one "I thought," a far from inconsiderable one: "I thought my friend Michael Lynch was dying *and I thought I was healthy*" (255, emphasis added). While I feel a bit sheepish revealing that I withheld such an important aspect of this passage, I take heart from the recognition that Sedgwick herself deferred this second surprise. Earlier I noted the repetition between the opening sentences of sections 2 and 4. Section 2 opens: "Four months ago when I decided to write 'White Glasses' for this conference I thought it was going to be an obituary for Michael Lynch." When she repeats nearly the same sentence to open section 4, the mistaken assumption has doubled.

"When I decided to write 'White Glasses' four months ago, I thought my friend Michael Lynch was dying and I thought I was healthy." The sentence structure emphasizes the parallel between these two mistaken assumptions. As the passage goes on, it continues this tight paralleling: "Michael didn't die; I wasn't healthy: within the space of a couple weeks, we were dealing with a breathtaking revival of Michael's energy, alertness, appetite — also with my unexpected diagnosis with a breast cancer already metastasized to several lymph nodes."

Shortly after deciding to write "White Glasses," Sedgwick learns she has cancer. While she reveals this in the paper, she only ever talks about this "unexpected diagnosis" in tandem with the other surprise, Michael's "breathtaking revival." "White Glasses," named for the glasses Sedgwick and Lynch both wore, is all about this pairing, about how they are together in this queer moment of the double surprise.

The framework for both surprises remains the ironic temporality of the writing of "White Glasses": "Unreflecting, I formed my identity as the prospective writer of this piece around the obituary presumption that my own frame for speaking . . . was the clearest thing in the world. In fact it was totally opaque: Michael didn't die; I wasn't healthy. . . . So I got everything wrong" (255). The self-irony is extreme: what looked like "the clearest thing in the world" turned out to be "totally opaque." The naïveté here scorned involves forming an "identity." It is a commonplace that queer theory, of the sort practiced by Sedgwick, involves a critique of identity. What we read here is indeed a critique of identity, but the identity in question is neither a sexual nor a gender identity—it is a writerly identity. Talking about the formation of her identity as "writer of this piece," she reveals the blindness of that identity—blindness that is bound up with a certain temporality, her identity as a "prospective writer."

While Sedgwick's reader cannot help but care about her diagnosis, about the fact of her having a life-threatening illness, I want nonetheless to try here and respect the particular frame in which she first narrates this event. I must confess that I am finding this hard to do, hard not to let the pathos of cancer overshadow her careful exposition of it in this tight ironic construction. That is certainly why I deferred this topic until I had established my framework; that is probably why Sedgwick deferred this same topic until she had established her framework.

I want to try to respect this framework, first of all by noting her insistence on the "frame": "I formed my identity . . . around the . . . presumption that my own *frame* for speaking . . . was the clearest thing in the world. In fact it was totally opaque" (emphasis added). The "frame" she is talking about is the frame for the paper she calls "White Glasses," but we should also connect that "frame" to the "white-framed glasses" themselves. The object she envied Lynch and resolved to find for herself, after all, was not literally white glasses but white frames.

Sedgwick repeats the word "frame" later in the same paragraph: "Now shock and mourning gaze in both directions through the obituary frame" (255–56). Although "the obituary frame" is the genre of writing she undertakes in "White Glasses," the "frame" here is quite explicitly something that can be "gazed through." The "obituary frame" is like a pair of glasses, like the white glasses that both Sedgwick and Lynch wear. The memorial mentions that "in many cultures white is the color of mourning" (255), which makes the glasses themselves a sort of "obituary frame."

Perhaps most importantly, this gaze goes "in both directions," as if Sedgwick and Lynch were sharing a single pair, looking at each other through the same glasses. This two-way gaze might recall the fantasy of reciprocal reading and writing we considered in the Owens memorial. In that earlier memorial, she imagines reading her own writing "through Craig's eyes"; in the second memorial, she wears glasses like Lynch's and feels she "see[s] with Michael's eyes." In 1990 Sedgwick mourns the loss of someone who is for her both an author and a reader, mourns the loss of a two-way relation of reading and writing. In this 1991 obituary, not only does she memorialize that two-way relation, she enacts it.

"White Glasses" tells us that in 1991 Michael Lynch, though himself dying, was very worried about Sedgwick's health. This obituary is not just Sedgwick mourning Lynch: "Shock and mourning gaze in both directions through the obituary frame." Seeing through Michael's eyes, writing with his glasses on, she prospectively mourns her own death.

Since Lynch is still alive, the mourning for him is likewise prospective, premature. Although Sedgwick will go on to live many years after Lynch dies, in this particular moment in early 1991, both find themselves in what Sedgwick will later — using the Tibetan Buddhist concept of the *bardo* as a transitional time — call "the bardo that extends from diagnosis until death."[30] Lynch and Sedgwick face each other in a very queer moment, neither dead yet but both facing death, each other's and their own.

By paralleling Lynch's non-death with her life-threatening condition, "White Glasses" places them together in a moment where the dead are not yet dead and the living no longer quite living. In Sedgwick's uncanny 1991 memorial, not only is the subject of the obituary disturbingly not yet dead, but the obituary is haunted by its writer's death. "White Glasses" is haunted by the death of its author.

The single dense, rich paragraph that is section 4 is where Sedgwick reveals to her reading public that she has cancer — advanced, metastasized, life-threatening. This revelation occurs within a paragraph that begins, "When I decided to write . . ." and that ends "it is full of stimulation and interest, even, to be ill and writing." She thus frames the advent of this life-threatening disease within a story of writing.

Sedgwick's diagnosis is inscribed in this text as a misfortune befalling the writer. The "unexpected diagnosis" is part of the ironic twist dividing the "prospective writer" from someone, in the present perfect, "writing." The threat to her life is located in the temporal gap that opens up between the prospective writer and writing. Her cancer is thus framed as a twist in the writer's fate. Indecent as it might seem, because I take Sedgwick as a theorist of writing's temporality, I read her "unexpected diagnosis" as a particularly dramatic example of a more general temporality of writing. And I notice that it repeats the twists in the tale of writing recounted in her "Memorial for Craig Owens." Like Owens's death, her cancer is an unexpected turn that interrupts her presumptions as prospective writer.

In the Owens memorial, Sedgwick is looking at death from within the writing experience, but it is the reader's death mourned there. But then, in the reciprocal relation she describes, the roles of reader and author might be interchangeable. A year later, Sedgwick is once again facing death while writing, but this time she can see herself as a dying writer. This time she writes under the threat of the author's death. In the introductory section of this chapter, while discussing Sedgwick's announcement of the queer moment in *Tendencies'* foreword, I intentionally left something out of a passage I was quoting. In the long italicized parenthesis that follows her saying "I suppose this must be called the moment of Queer," we find: "Long moment of a deathly silence. . . . When Melvin Dixon and Tom Yingling disappear from us, *and Audre Lorde*" (xii, emphasis added). I intentionally omitted the last three words of this quotation earlier. I went on to connect the two gay authors who died of AIDS in this sentence with Owens and Lynch, with the two gay writers memorialized in *Tendencies*. In that reading, Audre Lorde who died of metastasized breast cancer would be a placeholder for Sedgwick herself, a queer woman writer positioned with the men dying of AIDS. "What is at work here is an identification that falls across . . . the ontological crack between the living and the dead" ("White Glasses," 257). What is at work here in *Tendencies*'s queer moment is Sedgwick's identification with the dead author.

:: :: ::

"White Glasses" ends—and thus *Tendencies* ends—in a rather haunting way. The paper concludes with section 13 (itself an uncanny number): "A week ago . . . Michael and . . . I were talking about White Glasses . . . 'Are you going to record it for me?' [Michael asked.] So I am recording it. Hi Michael! I know I probably got almost everything wrong but I hope you didn't just hate this. See you in a couple of weeks" (266).

This was how the talk ended when presented on May 9, 1991. But as it appears in *Tendencies*, this final section is immediately followed by a one-line endnote in smaller font: "Michael Lynch died of AIDS on 9 July 1991." I find myself overly fascinated by the actual date—exactly 2 months after Sedgwick presents "White Glasses," almost exactly a year after Craig Owens died. While these numerical coincidences are not really meaningful, I think my fascination with them derives in part from the text's insistent focus on dates.

Like so many of the sections, the last one opens with a temporal index: "A week ago" (compare: "Four months ago," "It took me a year and a half"). But unlike the other sections, the thirteenth one also closes with a temporal marker, this one prospective. The section thus delimits precisely a present moment, between "a week ago" and "in a couple of weeks."

The final sentence of section 13—"See you in a couple of weeks"—finds a troubling echo in the endnote's announcement of Lynch's death "a couple of" months later. Yet, however disturbing we might find this juxtaposition between Lynch alive, with an immediate future, and the announcement of his death soon after, I think the inclusion of Lynch's death might ultimately make the published version less uncanny than the paper as presented on May 9, at least inasmuch as it normalizes the status of this obituary piece, turns it into what Sedgwick had originally planned to write—a memorial for someone who had already died.

By publishing the May 9 version of "White Glasses" unrevised in *Tendencies*, Sedgwick records the strange and unsettling moment of her obituary for a living friend, a moment whose fleetingness is borne home by the endnote. Rather than revise the talk so it would be a legitimate obituary, Sedgwick publishes it as it was, adding an endnote to allow us to feel how very fleeting that moment was.

I want here to connect this moment of May 9, 1991, with the moment in late July 1990 when Sedgwick makes us feel so poignantly her despair at finishing the essay she was hoping to send Owens. By including her memorial for Owens in *Tendencies*, she sets it up to be read in conjunction with the endnote to "Tales of the Avunculate," which informs the reader that, just a couple of months after proclaiming her despair at finishing the essay, she in fact finished it.

Tendencies includes two memorials, and their inclusion brings into the book not only her mourning for gay men dying of AIDS, but at the same time two stories of Sedgwick writing, each with a similar dramatic twist. More than that: because both memorials are occasional pieces, they also bring into the volume the conspicuous contrast between how things seemed in the poignant moment of the occasion and the way things had turned out by the time of publication. This contrast is part of the book's remarkable and insistent temporality.

In an interview with Barber and Clark done in 2000, Sedgwick says: "That's the wonderful thing about the printed word—it can't be updated instantly. It's allowed to remain anachronistic in relation to the culture of the moment."[31] What we see in the occasional, mourning pieces included in *Tendencies* is precisely Sedgwick's refusal to "update": she allows them to "remain anachronistic."

This gesture is a way of resisting what in the interview she calls "the culture of the moment." Ironically, Sedgwick resists "the culture of the moment" by holding to what I would in fact call "the moment." The foreword to *Tendencies* refers to this "culture of the moment" as "the short-shelf-life American marketplace of images" and sets it in direct opposition to the "moment": "In the short-shelf-life American marketplace of images, maybe the queer moment, if it's here today, will for that very reason be gone tomorrow. But I mean the essays collected in this book to make, cumulatively, stubbornly, a counterclaim against that obsolescence. . . . Queer is a continuing moment" (xii).

"Continuing moment" is quite a peculiar temporal concept (oxymoronic, I would say). I think it has something to do with how Sedgwick resists the "culture of the moment" by holding on to the moment in all its anachronism, refusing to update. Holding on—as in "White Glasses" with its "See you in a couple of weeks"—to the "today" that is here, despite the knowledge that it will be "gone tomorrow."

I connect this idea of the "continuing moment" with her comment in 2000 about how "the printed word can't be updated instantly." While this comment was made in the context of a discussion of AIDS and how to resist the amnesia that had already set in, its actual phrasing—"That's the wonderful thing about the printed word"—suggests that the statement might apply quite generally to writing and publishing. We might want to recognize the "continuing moment" as the temporality of the printed word.

What Sedgwick celebrates about "the printed word" is precisely what so many writers (myself included) fear—what in "the short-shelf-life marketplace" is called "obsolescence." It is in the context of talking about AIDS that Sedgwick embraces the anachronism of the printed word. A decade earlier, it is in the context of mourning gay men dying young that Sedgwick comes to value, not "the culture of the moment," not keeping up-to-date, but holding on to what has passed. It is this experience of mourning, I suspect, that transforms her relation to the temporality of writing.

Instead of being, as most of us are, embarrassed by the queer temporality of the printed word, Sedgwick would embrace and celebrate it. While the writer may go about revising and updating, the printed word is the province not of the writer but of the author. The printed word, necessarily anachronistic, is where the writer confronts her status as a dead author.

:: :: ::

April 2009: As I finished what I thought were my final revisions on this chapter, I learned that Eve Kosofsky Sedgwick had died.

Chapter 4

THE PERSISTENT AND VANISHING PRESENT

::

The previous chapter elaborated on Stephen Barber's and David Clark's notion of "queer temporality," applying it to the uncanny temporality of Sedgwick's memorial writing. While Barber and Clark derive their queer temporality from a reading of Sedgwick's corpus, in the very formulation of this temporality, they have occasion to refer to one other theorist, someone not generally considered a queer theorist: "What remains evident . . . across the entire body of [Sedgwick's] work, is another conception and unfolding of temporality, a specifically queer temporality. . . . This Sedgwick calls . . . 'a continuing moment,' the sort of persistent present formulated by Gayatri Chakravorty Spivak."[1]

This quotation includes two sentences from Barber's and Clark's "Queer Moments." Positing "another conception and unfolding of temporality," the first sentence here uses the phrase "queer temporality" for the first time ever. The second sentence quoted—the very next sentence after the first usage of "queer temporality"—explains Sedgwick's temporality by citing a formulation by Spivak. While I am, like Barber and Clark, impressed by the similarity between Sedgwick's and Spivak's temporalities, I am in fact more struck by the peculiar place of Spivak in their exposition. They seem to need Spivak to explain their idea of queer temporality, yet nowhere in their long essay do they ever mention Spivak again.

This fleeting reference suggests that Spivak's work has a place in the elaboration of queer temporality, and that we might want to bear in mind Barber's and Clark's notion as we read Spivak. The present chapter will follow up on this suggestion. Having outlined a queer temporality of writing in the last chapter, we will here proceed to look at the quite twisted temporality of Spivak's writing.

In their only reference to Spivak, Barber and Clark use the phrase "persistent present." This phrase is not itself a quotation but rather is constructed out of a longer phrase, which they quote at the end of the sentence ("a persistent effortfulness that makes a 'present'").[2] While not an actual quotation, this same "persistent present" appears again in the note Barber and Clark append to their citation of Spivak: "It cannot be without significance that both Spivak and Sedgwick, in different contexts, animate this persistent present in their work" (51 n. 2). Our reading of Spivak here will be very much devoted to this persistent present. I take up the phrase from Barber and Clark because I appreciate their sense of its queer temporality, but also because in my own reading of Spivak, I have noted her repeated emphasis on the persistent, the way that word regularly marks for Spivak a valued temporality.

Barber and Clark connect Spivak's "persistent present" to Sedgwick's "continuing moment." Our last chapter concluded by focusing on this oxymoronic phrase, which, I suggested, not only is queer ("Queer is a continuing moment") but is also the temporality of the printed word. Might Spivak's "persistent present" likewise indicate the temporality of the printed word?

Although the bulk of our previous chapter was concerned with Sedgwick's memorial texts, that chapter's conclusion moved on to consider a more general—less occasional, more theoretical—relation to the temporality of writing. It is in that context that we looked at the "continuing moment," at Sedgwick's queer persistent present, connecting it to her embrace of the anachronism of the printed word and the unavoidable obsolescence of the author.

This chapter continues where the previous one left off. In our reading of Spivak, we will be considering not the occasional moment of writing in confrontation with literal death, but rather the more general theoretical dilemma of writing in the shadow of obsolescence. As I concluded in the last chapter, the inevitable anachronism of the printed word is where the writer confronts her status as a dead author. This is the drama we will follow in Spivak's writing. Where Sedgwick writes in the shadow of death, facing not only the loss of friends but her own diagnosis with a life-threatening illness, it is not death that forces Spivak to imagine herself as a dead author; rather it is her attempt finally to write a book.

:: :: ::

In August 1986, Gayatri Chakravorty Spivak was interviewed in Australia by the *Melbourne Journal of Politics*. The interview is rich with theoretical ideas, political commitment, and wit; the discussion ranges widely through topics such as privilege, deconstruction, identity, and the vanguardism of theory. As the interview ends, Spivak is asked the stock closing question, "What are you doing now?" "Well, I'm supposedly revising a manuscript called 'Master Discourse, Native Informant: Deconstruction in the Service of Reading,'" she replies—and then she pauses (ellipsis in the text) and says: "I'm not a book writer, I'm very unhappy about the fact that I have finally had to perpetrate a book, but that's that."[3]

By 1986, Spivak is internationally known and widely influential, with the reputation to merit invitations to Australia and interviews in journals, but she has not yet written a book. She is working on her first book, "finally." Or not quite working on it—"*supposedly* revising a manuscript." Producing a book seems not what she has chosen but what she is forced to do—"had to" she says. Most strikingly, she uses the verb "perpetrate." The verb has a range of meanings, all pretty negative: from the first, most familiar meaning, "be guilty of (as a crime, an offense)," to "carry through (a deception)," to what is the most likely meaning in this context, "produce, perform, or execute badly or in a manner held to be execrable or shocking."[4] Criminal, fraudulent, or just shockingly bad—no wonder she is "very unhappy" about having to do it.

Although the title Spivak gave in this interview, "Master Discourse, Native Informant: Deconstruction in the Service of Reading," never in fact appeared on any book, the manuscript in question was published in 1999 (with substantial revision, to be sure) under the title *A Critique of Postcolonial Reason*. (While no longer appearing in the title, the concept of the "Native Informant" remains central in that book; "Deconstruction in the Service of Reading" becomes the title of the book's appendix.) Between the moment of this interview and the time *A Critique of Postcolonial Reason* appears, Spivak will actually publish two books, *In Other Worlds* (1987) and *Outside in the Teaching Machine* (1993)—not even counting the collection that includes the interview (*The Post-Colonial Critic*, 1990). None of these, however, qualify as perpetrating a book.

In the interview Spivak goes on to say: "I'm afraid of writing books, because I've found myself changing my mind so much, I don't particularly like what I write." She pauses again, then continues: "But nevertheless I think the time has come to take the plunge. And then there's a . . . collection of essays coming out—my old essays, indeed—and . . . it's called *In Other Worlds*" [ibid.]. When she says she's "afraid of writing books . . . but . . . the time has come to take the plunge," she is not, it seems, talking about the collection of her essays that is about to appear. That volume, first published in 1987, has recently been reissued in the Routledge Classics series—"books that have, by popular consent, become established as classics in their field."[5] Yet, however much Routledge or "popular consent" might consider *In Other Worlds* a book, Spivak in 1986 is distinguishing between books and collections of essays.[6]

The book that will become *A Critique of Postcolonial Reason* represents a dramatic departure for Spivak. It is, by her definition, her first book. "I'm afraid of writing books," she tells her interviewers, "but nevertheless I think the time has come to take the plunge."

The manuscript for *A Critique of Postcolonial Reason* is, in 1986, finished; she is not composing, merely revising. Or, rather, *supposedly* revising. Yet despite the pronouncement that "the time has come," we can hear her hesitation, her resistance to taking that plunge. While the language of "taking the plunge" and "the time has come" suggests immediate action, in fact this revision will take a dozen years. And while the book will finally be "perpetrated," just as the millennium is drawing to a close, the published book will be marked through and through by Spivak's fear and dislike of writing books. I propose in this chapter to read those marks in *A Critique of Postcolonial Reason*. Like her pronouncement that "the time has come," they speak of Spivak's confrontation with the temporality of writing books.

After Spivak says, "I'm not a book writer," her interviewers ask: "Is that a deliberate strategy, though? To be an essayist rather than a book writer?" Spivak replies: "I don't know that it's a deliberate strategy, it's possible that I've made a virtue out of necessity. I'm afraid of writing books" (48). While questioning the journal's attribution to her of a masterful, deliberate strategy, Spivak affirms that she has in fact been "an essayist rather than a book writer." We might understand this difference between "essayist" and "book writer" as the difference between writer and author. For Spivak, "the time has come" for her to be an author.

The difference between "essayist" and "book writer" at stake here plays out in the register of temporality; writer and author inhabit different temporalities. In Spivak's magnum opus, her attempt to perpetrate a book, we can read the marks of her encounter with the temporality of book writing, the temporality of authorship. I appreciate these marks as a contribution to theorizing authorship, as a prolonged and moving reflection on the dilemma of a writer all too aware of the necessary anachronism of the printed word, struggling with the fact that to be an author is inevitably to be a dead author, past not present.

:: :: ::

Earlier in the same 1986 interview—long before the final question of what she is "doing now"—Spivak has occasion to mention the temporality of writing books. It seems to come up quite gratuitously, where one would not expect it. I would like to consider the passage at length. Asked about the way she has challenged phallic metaphors, Spivak says, "One should perhaps clean up the metaphorical situation moment by moment, that is to say, in a certain *persistent* way." Picking up on her phrasing, the interviewers then ask, "Can we clean up metaphor?" to which she answers, "No. It's like cleaning teeth. You know, you will never be able to clean your teeth once and for all. But cleaning one's teeth, keeping oneself in order, etc.—*it's not like writing books*. You don't do these things once and for all. That's why it should be *persistent*" (41, emphasis added). Note Spivak's repeated use of "persistent" here. There are many examples of what is persistent ("keeping oneself in order, etc."), but when she wants an example of what is *not* persistent ("it's not like") what comes to mind is "writing books."

The *Journal of Politics* then responds, "So political practice is like housework?" and Spivak replies, "And who doesn't know this? Except political theorists who are opining from the academy with theological solutions *once and for all*. I mean, political practice is more complex than housework, but . . . it involves the same *persistent* effort" (41, emphasis added).

Spivak is here contrasting two modes of practice, and those two modes epitomize two different temporalities. One mode is "moment by moment," what she calls "persistent"; the other she characterizes as "once and for all." Her preference for the persistent mode is unmistakable. Political practice—like housework, like personal hygiene—is daily, repetitive, "moment by moment." It partakes of the common and the widespread ("who doesn't know this?" who doesn't clean their teeth?). In contrast with this common world of dailiness and repetition, we have "opining from the academy" and "theological solutions," operating in the temporality of "once and for all." Spivak's contempt for this academic and theological superiority is clear. And in the same "once and for all" boat with academic opining and theological solutions, she places "writing books."

At the beginning of the present chapter, following Barber's and Clark's suggestion, I imagined that Spivak's "persistent present" might be, like Sedgwick's queer "continuing moment," the temporality of the printed word. Here, however, as we read Spivak's deployment of "persistent," it would seem to be the very opposite of the temporality of writing books. Before trying to adjudicate this discrepancy, let us keep reading Spivak's articulation of the temporalities of writing.

"I'm afraid of writing books, because I've found myself changing my mind so much," she will say at the end of the same 1986 interview. A "moment by moment" temporality would better suit these frequent changes. "But nevertheless I think the time has come to take the plunge." In the phrase "the time has come" and in the figure "taking the plunge," we hear Spivak's resolve to submit to the "once and for all" temporality — a temporality that she not only fears but that she objects to, politically and theoretically.[7]

We can find a hint of her theoretical and political objection to books in the second chapter of *A Critique of Postcolonial Reason*. Pausing in the middle of her reading of Baudelaire, Spivak comments on what she is doing: "Here I use the resources of deconstruction 'in the service of reading' to develop a strategy (rather than a theory) of reading matching the situation of reading that might lead to a literary critique of imperialism, although its very inclusion in the covers of a book courts its effacement or neutralization as strategy."[8]

This sentence is a self-conscious, "meta," moment in the book. Beginning with "Here," it ends by questioning the effect of including what she is doing "in the covers of a book" (one possible meaning of "here"). The sentence distinguishes between a "strategy" and a "theory" of reading; at stake in the distinction may be the same two temporal modes we saw in the 1986 interview. While theories strive to be "once and for all," strategies belong to the "moment by moment." A strategy (unlike a theory) would "match the situation." Once again the stakes for such a temporal mode are political: if she can develop a situational strategy, then that "might lead to a literary critique of imperialism." If strategy, unlike theory, is situational, moment-by-moment, inclusion in a book risks undoing that temporality, turning the strategy into a theory, making it "once and for all."

In this sentence from the second chapter we recognize the old 1986 subtitle, "deconstruction in the service of reading." While that phrase continues to have a certain prominence in the published book, the subtitle we now find on the cover is "Toward a History of the Vanishing Present." I don't know if the idea of "the vanishing present" is meant to connect to the publication date at the very end of the millennium, but I take this subtitle as evidence for the importance of temporality in the 1999 book, in the book as it appears after a dozen years of revision. And, as my title for the present chapter suggests, I want to ponder the relation between this "vanishing present" and what Barber and Clark call the persistent present.

The preface to *A Critique of Postcolonial Reason* tells us that "the text seeks to catch the vanishing present" (x). The evocative "vanishing present" that we encounter first in the subtitle on the cover of the book must be understood within this relation. The "text"—by which she means the book she is prefacing—is trying to, wants to, "catch" the present. The present is the book's object of desire: elusive, fleeting—i.e., vanishing. The book is motivated by this pursuit of the present, but there is a sense of extreme difficulty—futility even—in seeking to catch something "vanishing." In a footnote to the fourth and final chapter of *Postcolonial Reason*, Spivak in fact writes, "We cannot keep up with the vanishing present" (339).

While this might sound like not only an announcement of futility but also a giving up, throwing in the towel, nevertheless a look at the note that includes this sentence reveals in a more detailed way the book's relation to the vanishing present. The note appears during a discussion of the Japanese fashion house *Comme des Garçons*. Discussing it as an example of transnationalization, Spivak writes: "'Under which country's law is this?' It looks like, in 1984, the buildings were Bank of New York and the merchandise Tokyo's Fuji Bank." Right after "Fuji Bank," the superscript number 39 directs us to a footnote dense with marks of the book's temporality: "These are the laws that, as the morning news in New York City reports on 12 Mar. 1998, are making Japanese entrepreneurs hang themselves. We cannot keep up with the vanishing present. Readers will remember that time as the era when finance capital came crashing down in the Asia-Pacific" (339).

There is a lot going on here; I will nonetheless restrict my remarks to the note's densely layered temporality. The text proper refers to "in 1984"; this discussion of *Comme des Garçons* is a reading of a 1984 *Village Voice* article. Spivak's text (in contradistinction to the note) was part of the manuscript already written by the time of the 1986 interview.[9] Whereas the text refers to 1984 and dates from the mid-eighties, the footnote refers to March 12, 1998, and was presumably written on that very date. The note, written more than a dozen years later, is a gesture toward bringing the material in the text up to date.

With its talk of "the morning news . . . reports," the footnote sounds the tone of what television news likes to call "late breaking," which is all about updating, trying to catch the present.[10] In an essay on historiography published in 1985, Spivak advocates a "historical sense" which, she says, is "much like a newscaster's persistently revised daily bulletin."[11] (Note the "persistent" here.) While she gets the phrase "historical sense" from Michel Foucault, Spivak fleshes it out with the image of the newscaster's bulletin.[12] Foucault's sense of history might be particularly relevant to her 1999 book: the phrase "history of the present" in *Postcolonial Reason*'s subtitle comes from Foucault (Spivak adds "vanishing").[13] In place of the "arrogance" of traditional history that from an overview perspective can put events into a continuous development, Spivak's essay on historiography recommends the "newscaster's persistently revised daily bulletin" as "a strategy for our times" ("Subaltern Studies," 285). In this text published a year before the *Melbourne Journal of Politics* interview, we find again the contrast between an arrogant, superior temporality (in this case, traditional history) and the strategic temporality of daily effort that, based on this quotation, we might call "persistent revision."

This persistent revision recalls the phrase Barber and Clark quote from Spivak—"a persistent effortfulness that makes a 'present.'" Persistent revision is the persistent present as a practice of, as well as a temporality of, writing. The very opposite of Sedgwick's embrace of the anachronism of the printed word, it entails a vigilant struggle against that anachronism. Persistent revision is "a strategy for our times"—i.e., a strategy to resist the present's vanishing, a strategy to catch a vanishing present.

In the March 12, 1998, note to *Postcolonial Reason*, it is, ironically, right after she gives us the very latest from the morning news that Spivak says, "We cannot keep up with the vanishing present." However persistently we might revise, we cannot keep up. The pronouncement of futility seems to refer not as much to the updating news-bulletin sentence that precedes it as to the sentence that follows: "Readers will remember that time as the era when finance capital came crashing down in the Asia-Pacific." Note the tense of this sentence's verbs. As she moves to the future when we will read her, the present of the footnote's first sentence ("as the morning news reports") moves into the past tense ("came crashing down"). In the space of this short note, the present vanishes into the past.

This footnote dates a present (March 12, 1998), which is contrasted not only with a past ("in 1984") but also with a future (a moment that will see March 1998 as a past "era"). This note is an encounter with the temporality of books, the temporality of authorship. The past is the moment of writing (years before publication); the future is the anticipated moment of reading; the present is when the author adds a note to try and update the text at the last moment before publication.

More than a dozen years after drafting the text, Spivak makes a final attempt to bring things up-to-date, yet she is at the very same time acutely aware that, once published, the text will become out-of-date for future readers. Her persistent present becomes, in this very note that would contribute to its persistence, nonetheless a vanishing present. As the author imagines her future readers, she imagines our present, one that relegates her to the past; in the future she foresees, the author, as the saying goes, "is history."

:: :: ::

Later in the final chapter, we find another footnote that refers to "attempting to catch a vanishing present." This note is nearly a page long, and the reference to catching a vanishing present is at the very end of the note. The text is discussing Marshall McLuhan's 1989 book *The Global Village* (this was, presumably, not part of the 1986 manuscript). After saying that McLuhan's book "is an impassioned song of praise for the Bell Telephone System and AT&T," Spivak appends a footnote that begins by talking about "western supremacist prophets of technology," quotes at some length from a 1997 article by Richard Rorty, goes on to mention that the AT&T compound that was bombed at the 1996 Olympics was called "The Global Village," and then mentions Rorty again, this time coupled with Samuel Huntington, saying they would "scrap the civilizing-mission-cum-global-villagizing alibi altogether."[14] There are obviously a lot of different things on which we might comment here, but I want only to give a quick overview of this bulky, rambling note. After the sentence about Rorty and Huntington, the footnote finally comes to an end with two sentences reflecting on the temporality of the book in which it appears: "To note this no longer anticipates my argument in this chapter. It transforms books such as this one, narrative footnotes and all, into the memorabilia of a previous conjuncture, attempting to catch a vanishing present" (367).

This is a dense, complicated, substantive note; I will restrict my discussion to the final two sentences. While I am not sure whether the "this" in "To note this" refers to the previous sentence, to some portion of the previous sentence, to something else earlier in the note, or to the entire note, it does seem clear that these two sentences are not just what I earlier called a "meta" moment in the book; they actually constitute a meta-footnote. They add commentary on the note itself, rather than on the text, even commenting on the book's footnotes more generally.

"To note this no longer anticipates my argument in this chapter." While this is a short and (except for the antecedent to "this") relatively simple sentence, it has a somewhat complex temporality. "No longer anticipates": the phrase involves pastness and futurity, though not in the usual linear relation. At some point in the past, this note, or part of this note, *anticipated* the chapter's argument, looked forward to or even jumped ahead to an argument that had not yet been made (or at least appeared later in the book). Anticipation is a relation to futurity. But this note "no longer anticipates"; the future it looked forward to will now never come; the note's anticipated future has vanished into the past.

The specific temporal references of this "no longer anticipates" are even more puzzling than its twisted past-future. By implying that at some point in the book's genesis, this note, or something in this note, anticipated the chapter's argument, it suggests that at least some part of the note was drafted earlier than the final two sentences, that the meta-note was added to update the note. Here we are no longer in the simple time frame of mid-eighties text versus late nineties revision (the time frame we have been following so far in the present chapter). While the last two sentences seem to suggest that (at least some part of) the note was drafted before the final version of the chapter's argument, the note with its reference to a 1996 event and to a text published in 1997 seems itself to have been drafted (at least in part) rather late in the revision process. Though I don't feel able to create a time line here (as I could for the note we looked at earlier), I have an even stronger sense of the note's temporality as layered, of the note as having been written in several different moments, of the note as multiply, indeed persistently, revised.

"It transforms books such as this one, narrative footnotes and all, into the memorabilia of a previous conjuncture, attempting to catch a vanishing present." The final sentence of the footnote not only comments on this note but also expands the commentary to apply to such notes in general, to the book as a whole, and even to the whole category, "books such as this one." To explain what she means by the latter category, Spivak apposes the phrase "narrative footnotes and all." The lengthy footnote in which this phrase appears is hardly unique; in fact it is far from the longest such note in the book. Spivak calls these "narrative footnotes," suggesting that they don't just give information but tell some sort of story, that they put information in a temporally unfolding sequence. "And all" implies that there are other things in the same category as the narrative footnotes, other things that work like they do. Indeed it is not only in the footnotes that we find such marks of persistent revision: they also appear in the text, sometimes in paragraph-long parentheses trying to update, and even sometimes not parenthetically, as the main text explicitly goes back and forth between earlier and later versions. Along with the narrative footnotes, these are all part of the attempt "to catch the vanishing present."

This note's take on that attempt is even more pessimistic than the note 30 pages earlier with its admission that "we cannot keep up with the vanishing present." Here not only do we not keep up, but the very attempt, "narrative footnotes and all," has been transformed into the "memorabilia of a previous conjuncture." It seems that the very attempts to catch the present may be precisely what turn such books into quaint, antiquated souvenirs.

This meta-footnote to Spivak's 1999 book reminds me of a remark by Sedgwick that we considered at the close of our previous chapter. "That's the wonderful thing about the printed word," says Sedgwick in a 2000 interview, "it can't be updated instantly. It's allowed to remain anachronistic in relation to the culture of the moment."[15] I connect Sedgwick's "anachronistic in relation to the culture of the moment" to Spivak's "memorabilia of a previous conjuncture."[16] Where Sedgwick celebrates the anachronism, Spivak—likewise finding it inevitable—sounds bitter about it. Although their affective tone might be diametrically opposed, the two writers share a sense of the temporality of "the printed word." Because "it can't be updated," it cannot help but become anachronistic.

Updating is precisely what Spivak's "narrative footnotes" are all about. While the coda appended to an already overlong footnote halfway through her last chapter declares the futility of such updating notes, the book begins by sounding much more hopeful about their usage. Since Spivak persists in using such notes, since they typify the peculiar temporality of her authorship, I do not want to take the moment of exasperation as definitive. Although the exasperation, the sense of futility, is part of the book's temporality, it must be understood alongside Spivak's continual revision. Spivak's writing present is, to be sure, vanishing, but it is also, nonetheless, persistent.

This persistence with regard to a vanishing present is seen in the second paragraph of the book's preface, which introduces the reader to the "narrative footnotes" and to the idea of "the vanishing present." Spivak explains: "My book charts a practitioner's progress from colonial discourse studies to transnational cultural studies. The latter position, a 'moving base' that I stand on as the text seeks to catch the vanishing present, has asserted itself in narrative footnotes. Some will find this irritating and confusing; some, *I hope*, will share the challenge" (ix–x, emphasis added). While there are no doubt readers who find her long notes "irritating and confusing," I may be one of the readers Spivak was hoping for: I certainly feel moved by "the challenge" of reading the footnotes, compelled by the drama of "seeking to catch the vanishing present."

When she started this book she was doing "colonial discourse studies," analyzing texts from the era when Europe was colonizing much of the world; by the time she publishes the book she has moved from discourse studies to cultural studies (looking at nonlinguistic as well as linguistic objects) and from focusing on the colonial period to focusing on the contemporary moment of transnationality. Her *Critique of Postcolonial Reason* might thus be said to frame the postcolonial, to frame it temporally, progressing from the colonial that precedes it to the transnational that follows it (while at the same time eagerly showing repetitions and similarities between the colonial and the transnational).

"The latter position, a 'moving base' that I stand on as the text seeks to catch the vanishing present, has asserted itself in narrative footnotes." Referring back to the previous sentence, "the latter position" is "transnational cultural studies"; transnational cultural studies is to be found in the narrative footnotes—for example, the remarks about Japanese entrepreneurs hanging themselves in 1998 or about the 1996 Olympic bombing. More striking is the phrase "has asserted itself," suggesting that transnational cultural studies has a will of its own, that it—rather than the author—speaks in the footnotes. The most remarkable part of this sentence is, to be sure, the parenthetic remark (set off in commas) that occupies its middle. Here is where we find "the text seek[ing] to catch the vanishing present"; as the text does that, the author "stands on" transnational cultural studies. Spivak's image of "standing" tropes on the "foot" of the footnotes: there is a pun here on the notes' position at the bottom—or "base"—of the page. What she is standing on is her "base," but unlike our usual notion of foundations it is a "moving base," which means that even as she is "standing" (which usually connotes a stationary position) she is in fact moving, allowing her to chase after "the vanishing present."[17]

The phrase "moving base" is in quotation marks because it is quoted from Foucault. Spivak first fixes on this two-word phrase in an essay she published in 1992.[18] In her 1992 essay, Spivak says that "moving base" is a "catachrestic concept-metaphor," meaning that it is an abusive figure of speech that precisely through its abuse is able to formulate a concept that would be lost in more standard language.[19] The abuse here is that we expect a base to be stationary; "moving base" seems a contradiction in terms. In Spivak's 1999 preface, the phrase is connected to the attempt to catch the present, to that aspect of the book represented by the book's subtitle. Since the subtitle alludes to Foucault's phrase "history of the present," this redeployment of "moving base" reinforces the importance of Foucault as a theoretical guide, a precursor for the book's "historical sense," for the book's attempt to catch the vanishing present.

"Moving base" is an important concept-metaphor for Spivak. The image of "standing on a 'moving base'" reappears in the middle of the last chapter, again in relation to the vanishing present: "This chapter is, after all, one woman teetering on the *socle mouvant* of the history of the vanishing present" (359). *Socle mouvant* is the French phrase from Foucault that gets translated as "moving base." The verb "teetering" emphasizes how very difficult it would be to stand on a moving base.[20]

I take Spivak's image of herself *standing on a moving base as the text seeks to catch the vanishing present* as an image of writing in time. Especially as enhanced by the last chapter's "teetering," the image represents the awkwardness and insecurity, the difficulty of writing in time. I would contrast this quite striking image with the very traditional explanation of the author's encounter with temporality that we find in the sentence immediately preceding the image's first appearance in the book. Just before the preface shows us the author standing on a moving base trying to catch the present, Spivak says, "My book charts a practitioner's progress." The sense of authorial possession in the phrase "my book" is a pretty far cry from the awkward "'moving base' that I stand on as the text seeks" where the author is only vaguely conjoined to "the text," where the text seems to have a will of its own. When Spivak says "my book," she also says "progress."[21] "Progress" does not seem like a word one would expect Spivak to use. The word "progress" generally denotes the most triumphant relation to temporality. "Progress" here represents the least troubled or troubling, the most positive version of a writer's change over time.[22]

This account of the author's movement in time is simple and clear, under control and reassuring, and that is probably why Spivak repeats it—literally quotes this very sentence—at the beginning of the first chapter. "This book is a 'practitioner's progress from colonial discourse studies to transnational cultural studies'" (2). Quoting this phrase would seem to give it authority, perhaps making it into an authoritative version of what is going on in this book. Appearing in the preface and then again at the beginning of the first chapter, this account of the book's trajectory is made available as a thumbnail sketch for the reader. Yet this handy, portable description is in fact quite atypical of the book, representing an authorial control and a version of temporality that is persistently undermined, including in the very passage where "progress" first appears—and again in the context where, as a quotation, it reappears.

The sentence where Spivak quotes from her preface is part of a longer footnote, one of the first notes to the first chapter, one of the very first narrative footnotes of the book. The note is particularly rich with marks of authorial temporality, and so I would like to consider it at some leisure.

On the second page of the first chapter, we find the note appended to the end of the following sentence: "It is beyond the scope of this book to demonstrate how the new North-South divide in the post-Soviet world imposes new limitations, although my argument will constantly seek to escape that caution" (2). Before we proceed to the note, let us remark that there is quite a bit going on in this sentence from the text. While the dominant imagery of the sentence may be spatial ("beyond the scope"), it also involves temporality ("the *new* North-South divide," "the *post*-Soviet World," "*new* limitations"). What is "beyond the scope" is in fact "the new." The "new" here is "post-Soviet," that is, post-1989. The fall of the Soviet Union not only moves the world from an East-West to a North-South divide, but according to Spivak also moves us into the era of transnationality; it inaugurates the present conjuncture, the era the book is progressing toward. What is at stake here, I think, is the challenge to the book posed by the fall of the Soviet Union, a world-changing event that occurs between the manuscript's original completion in the mid-eighties and its publication in 1999.

It is, to be sure, relatively conventional at the beginning of a book to mark off what is beyond the book's scope. What she says at the end of the sentence, however, is much less conventional. Her delineation of the book's scope is not a static, once-and-for-all mapping, but in fact a persistent tension: "My argument will constantly seek to escape that caution." The word "escape" suggests that the author, or at least her "argument," experiences the boundaries of the book's topic as imprisoning.

At the end of this sentence, a superscript 3 sends the reader to the bottom of the page where we find a note that continues, and complicates, the sentence's already pretty dramatic authorial meta-commentary on the book:

> This sentence was written at the start of the final revision, itself dislocated by the author's current active shuttling between North and South. This book is a "practitioner's progress from colonial discourse studies to transnational cultural studies." I report, therefore, that, in the last chapter . . . my reach exceeded my grasp and the caution gave way. The footnotes got longer, more narrative, pushing into the text.

The footnote repeats the word "caution" from the sentence in the text. The "caution" is another, more dramatic name for "the scope of this book," or for the recognition that something is "beyond the scope of this book." "Caution" makes the limits of the book seem like a dangerous edge, a precipice with danger signs posted. She goes on to specify that what happened when "the caution gave way" was that the footnotes got out of control. Not only did they get longer and more narrative, but they "pushed into the text." This last image suggests the footnotes got so big (and so "narrative") that they could no longer remain on the edge of the text; they breached the text's boundaries.[23] This is itself said in a footnote, one that while not really long is definitively narrative, what may in fact be the first narrative note of the book.

The footnote begins by locating us in the temporality of revision. The sentence in the text, the one that asserts and resents the limited scope of the book, was, we are told, "written at the start of final revision." The past tense "*was* written" tells us that this note itself dates from some time later than "the start of final revision," further into that revision. While the sentence in the text is late in the process of making this book (final revision), the footnote is even later, in a temporality we might call persistent revision.

Sometime after its start, the final revision is "dislocated." While "dislocate" is a spatial term, it affects the temporality of the book, opening a gap between the start of final revision and the end. Spivak refers to herself here as "the author." She calls herself "the author" as she experiences a dislocation, a gap between herself writing in the present and her previous writing now consigned to the past.

We saw something similar in my last chapter when Sedgwick, prefacing a new edition of *Between Men*, refers to herself as "the author of this book."[24] Writing at a temporal remove from that "author," she even refers to herself at one point as "the young author of this book." Sedgwick uses the name "author" for herself in a past moment, as she speaks at some distance from that past self. Spivak, in the footnote we are considering, likewise calls herself "the author" as she grapples with her past writing, as if the writer only becomes "the author" when her writing is in the past, as if the author is somehow the writer past. It is just after Spivak refers to herself as "the author" that she sounds most authorial, quoting the sentence from the preface about how "my book charts a progress." Yet, however conventionally authorial the quoted sentence might be, the footnote proceeds to a temporality that undoes any notion of progress. The third sentence of the note "reports" in the present tense about what happened "in the last chapter."[25] The reader is just beginning the first chapter; the author speaks to the reader from the last chapter. The sentence in the text, written at the start of final revision, tells us that her "argument *will . . . seek* to escape that caution"; the note, written some time later, tells us that "in the last chapter . . . the caution *gave way*." As we move from text to note, we jump from a future to a past tense. The text talks about the book in the future tense, as if it lies before us; the note, on the other hand, talks about the book in the past tense. The note where Spivak calls herself "the author" puts her book, her writing, in the past.

Encountered at the beginning of the first chapter, this note not only makes the reader feel out of sync with the author, but makes our sense of a present moment in the book vanish. This first narrative footnote thrusts the reader into the quest for the vanishing present, not just the present moment of culture or history, but also the present moment of reading. This first narrative footnote pushes the reader off the edge into the book's twisted and troubling temporality.

:: :: ::

"This book is a 'practitioner's progress from colonial discourse studies to transnational cultural studies.' I report, *therefore*, that, in the last chapter . . . the caution gave way. The footnotes got longer, more narrative, pushing into the text" (emphasis added). Part of the progress narrative here is the idea that the author's development over time is represented in the book's development from the first to the last chapter. Unlike the first three chapters where "the caution" held, it is only in the last that "the caution gave way." The last chapter is where the footnotes not only got longer and more narrative but they pushed into the text—where the sort of thing that should have remained on the margins moved into the text proper.

Now, to be sure, this account of the book makes sense. You might have noticed that many of the passages I have considered here do indeed come from the last chapter. Yet still I would say that things are not so neat as this progress narrative makes it seem. There are some very long narrative footnotes to be found in the first three chapters; the notes in the last chapter are neither definitively longer nor more narrative than those in earlier chapters. And we could also say that the sort of temporal layering of the book, the persistent updating that is a typical effect of the notes, can in fact be found not only in many of the early notes but likewise "pushing into the text" long before the final chapter.

Consider, for example, this moment from the first chapter: "I keep wanting to write this section differently," Spivak confides (in the body of the text, not in a footnote). The verb phrase here ("keep wanting") bespeaks the persistence of an urge to revise.

She then proceeds to sketch out how she would write the section differently: "One way *would* be to begin with a citation. . . . Next a reading . . . I *would* expand this . . . I *would* describe . . . I *would* cite" (67–70, emphasis added; since I only want to show the structure of this sketch of an alternative, I am not including the substantive material; suffice it to say that the version she sketches would update so as to take into account the transnational present). We might also remark that this alternative version includes a rich narrative footnote itself over a page long. After three pages the reverie of an alternative version ends thus: "But I can do no more than leave this mark of that possible . . . for it is too late to undertake so radical a rewriting" (70).[26] Spivak then proceeds with a short one-sentence paragraph, "Here, then, is the earlier text," and we go on to read a text now marked as "earlier," out-of-date.

This three-page sketch of a possible alternative opens the last section of chapter 1. The section will go on for 40 pages, but before we even get into her argument, we are forewarned that the author is not satisfied with it, that she wishes she had the time to revise it radically. This is in fact not the only time in this section that she will fantasize out loud how she could update—for example, in parentheses, "(If I were writing this section today, I would . . .)" (103). I find it, however, particularly remarkable that she does this before she begins her argument, thus marking it as obsolete before we even read it, consigning it to the past at the moment it lies ahead for the reader.

Chapter 1, "Philosophy," is broken into three numbered sections; the third and last section is devoted to Marx (the first two sections contain readings of, respectively, Kant and Hegel). Opening with this fantasy of what she "keeps wanting to write," section 3 actually begins with one additional sentence before what I quoted above: "Marx keeps moving for a Marxist as the world moves. I keep wanting to write this section differently. One way would be to begin with a citation from *The Communist Manifesto* . . ." (67). The "keep" of the author's "I keep wanting" repeats the "keeps" of "Marx keeps moving." Her persistence is a repetition of Marx's persistence. The "moving" in the first sentence, the double "moving . . . moves," might recall the image of the "moving base." Since Spivak is a Marxist, Marx could be called her "base."

"Marx keeps moving" is in itself a striking statement. Its present tense, its "keeps," its "moving," makes Marx alive, in the present, not stuck in the nineteenth century, the era of "colonial discourse." Marx here is something that might, along with the author, progress from colonial discourse to transnational culture. If the author only had the time, she could bring Marx into the present. While the book's present is "post-Soviet," it need not be post-Marxist, need not be post-Marx.

Marx keeps moving for a Marxist as the world moves. I keep wanting to write. . . . While these words appear in a book published in 1999, I would insist on their persistent, *still persistent*, present tense. Seven years after the publication of *The Critique of Postcolonial Reason*, Spivak says: "In 1978 I taught my first course on Marx. . . . I have written many pieces on Marx, too many to list here. A book on the possibility of socialist ethics has been brewing in my mind for all these years. The book changes its shape under my feet as history writes itself a present."[27]

The book changes its shape under my feet as history writes itself a present. This is a different "book" Spivak is talking about here in 2006, not *Postcolonial Reason*, another book, but we recognize the figure that represents her position as its author: standing on something that is not stationary, uncertain footing.[28] We also see here once again a relation between the moving base ("changing under my feet") and the "present," a relation that suggests that uncertain footing is a spatial figure for a temporal dilemma, a concept-metaphor to represent the writer's grappling with temporality, the situation of the author all too aware of writing in time.

:: :: ::

The Marx section of *Postcolonial Reason* opens with the assertion that "Marx keeps moving." Thirty pages later, in the middle of the section, Spivak says that Marx "keeps (us) going" (98). "Keeps going" repeats both the movement and the persistence of "Marx keeps moving"; the parenthetical "us" doubles the meaning so that Marx not only persists himself, but he underwrites, supports our own persistent movement (another version of Marx as "moving base"). While I would stress the similarity to "Marx keeps moving" at the beginning of the section, I must tell you that the Marx that keeps going on page 98 is actually a ghost.

A ghost is persistent. A ghost is dead but nonetheless remains — someone who has vanished but is nonetheless still there, something that both persists and vanishes. Whatever temporal logic allows something to be both persistent and vanishing, it is the logic of ghosts, the temporality of ghosts.

In relation to Marx, the ghost is a figure used by Spivak and Derrida in the mid-nineties in response to claims that Marx is dead in the "post-Soviet" world.[29] Subsequent to *Postcolonial Reason*, the ghost will become a very important figure in Spivak's work (see, for example, the ghost dance and the wish to be haunted in the 2003 *Death of a Discipline*). In the particular passage we are considering, however, the ghost derives specifically from Spivak's treatment of Marx *as an author*.

The ghost on page 98 of *Postcolonial Reason* is an explicit and direct response to the trope of the "death of the author." Spivak cites Roland Barthes's infamous phrase in order to situate her own reading practice. She says that deconstructive reading — the reading she practices, the reading she recommends — while including the kind of "deicide/parricide" represented by Barthes's phrasing, always combines and offsets that author-murder with "complicity." It is in order to explain the mixture of violence and complicity that constitutes the relation to the author in her practice of reading that she writes, "Even if we question the authority of Marx, his ghost keeps (us) going."

Spivak understands Barthes's "death of the author" as a refusal of the author's "authority." While she certainly joins Barthes in that anti-authoritarian reading, she counterbalances Barthes with the recognition that it is the author who keeps us going. Marx's ghost is Spivak's elaboration on, revision of, "the death of the author." Spivak's take on the author's death is consistent with her preference for persistence over the temporality of once-and-for-all. It does not deny that the author is dead, but it refuses that death any finality. *The author is dead but his ghost keeps (us) going.*

Ghosts are the dead returning. In the first chapter, we saw that Barthes in fact followed the polemical assertion of the author's death by a sense of his return.[30] Marx's ghost is Spivak's version of the return of the dead author.

At the end of my first chapter, we found Barthes talking about a "return of the author" in which the author who returns from the dead "goes into our life," where the first person plural ("our") implies readers.[31] I see the same first person plural when Spivak says that Marx's ghost "keeps *us* going." In talking about the return of the dead author, Barthes also introduces the idea of the reader "living with an author," which he calls a "co-existence." That "co-existence" might be bodied forth in Spivak's parenthetical "(us)" where Marx "keeps (us) going." The effect of the parenthesis is to make Marx's keeping going inseparable from his keeping us going, to make the author's continued existence inseparable from the way he affects the reader's existence.

Spivak's ghost takes us back to where we were at the end of my first chapter, with a sense of the author as dead but still with us, with the reader. The ghost shows us that the author of *Postcolonial Reason* was in fact thinking about the death of the author. Speaking as a reader, Spivak finds the author's ghost not troubling but enabling: he keeps us going. That ghost is, however, a more disturbing figure for her as a writer, for her as an author.

Let us again compare the ghost who "keeps (us) going" to the opening of the Marx section thirty pages earlier: "Marx keeps moving for a Marxist as the world moves. I keep wanting to write this section differently. . . . But . . . it is too late to undertake so radical a rewriting" (67–70). In the sentence with the parenthetic "(us)," Spivak and Marx both, together, "keep going." While these earlier sentences also link Marx's persistent movement to something persistent about Spivak (by means of the repeated "keep's"), here she only persists in her frustration, her discontent. On page 98, Spivak's "us" is a reader; on page 67, her "I" is an author. While the reader can join Marx in persistent movement, when she speaks as author, she only persists in wanting to revise, in being dissatisfied with her book, in wanting to bring it up to date while being unable to do so. Marx keeps moving; the world keeps moving; Spivak the author is stuck with writing she herself finds out-of-date, belated, obsolete.

I read the Marx who "keeps moving" as the same figure as the ghost who "keeps going" thirty pages later. The Marx on page 67 is not yet called a ghost, but he will be. While it is only when she speaks as a reader that Spivak explicitly treats Marx as a dead-but-still-going author, it is here where she speaks as a writer, here where she speaks as the book's author, that Marx's ghostlike uncanny persistence is connected to her frustration at not being able to bring her book up-to-date. It is precisely this connection between the dead author and the impossible quest for an up-to-date book that is my topic in the present chapter.

The figure of the ghost revitalizes Marx, making him while still dead also in some way alive, so the long-dead writer can keep moving, keep going. Spivak, on the other hand, while still literally alive cannot keep moving; she is stuck in a prior version of the book, stuck in the past, cannot bring the book into the present. ("It is too late to undertake so radical a rewriting. . . . Here, then, is the earlier text" [70].) The ghost resonates, ironically, with the fact that, while still alive, as an author Spivak is already immobile, past not present; while still alive, as an author Spivak is also already "dead." Although the possibility of being at once alive and dead may be good news for the nineteenth-century writer, it is not as happy a fate for the still living author.

:: :: ::

While Marx's ghost is a figure Spivak uses to make a general point about authors, it is probably not coincidental that Spivak talks about the death of the author in the section of her book on Marx. Marx is not just one of the authors Spivak reads; he is a model for her as an author.

In the final paragraph of her big book, her first book, Spivak returns one last time to the drama of her revision: "I have . . . let myself be encountered by that other book that I have had to keep pushing away while I have revised this one" (421).[32] She then asks the reader: "Please decide . . . if one can stitch together Kant's *Third Critique* and documents like *Chinta*." Kant's third critique (*The Critique of Judgment*) is the text she reads in the first part of the first chapter, where *Postcolonial Reason* begins. Toward the end of her last chapter she cites articles published in 1995 and 1996 (in Bengali) in the journal *Chinta* on Asian child labor. Her reading of Kant is part of the original project for this book (colonial discourse studies); her reading of *Chinta* belongs to "that other book" she would have written had she started the project in the late 1990s (transnational cultural studies). Rather than a "progress" from one to the other, we see here a conflict: she has to push away "that other book" in order to revise, in order to finish "this one." Rather than a seamless progress, the most she can hope for would be to stitch them together.

And it is here as she ends her book, wondering if it can possibly be one book, that Marx makes a final appearance. Following her question about the possibility of stitching together Kant and *Chinta*, the next sentence, the very last sentence of the book, reads: "Marx could hold *The Science of Logic* and the Blue Books together; but that was still only Europe; and in the doing it came undone."

Marx brought together his reading of Hegel's *Science of Logic* and of the "Blue Books" where he found labor statistics. Although I am not a scholar of Marx, I can see these represent two different kinds of texts, the same two represented by the contrast between the third critique and *Chinta*. Closing her book by asking if it is possible to stitch together the book's two conflicting directions, Spivak says that Marx "could hold" the two together.

Asking whether what she is trying to do in her book is possible, she answers that Marx did it. Of course, she then goes on to say why what she is doing is even harder: he was "only" looking at Europe while she is reading back and forth (shuttling) between the North and the South.[33] And then, even beyond the greater difficulty of her global scope, there is the final assessment, "in the doing it came undone."

This "coming undone" connects to the image of "stitching together." It is not clear here in the last sentence exactly what she is referring to. I connect this "doing" to her saying, sixty pages earlier, "Marx's books were not enough and the text of his doing remained caught in the squabbles of preparty formation and the vicissitudes of personal life" (368). While this connection suggests that the "doing" refers to activism beyond books ("books were not enough"), I would nonetheless say that, given the context of the paragraph in which her last sentence appears, Spivak is also talking about the "doing" of a book, of her book, which in the doing came undone.

In her final statement as author of her book, Spivak recalls Marx. Her enterprise, she tells us, is like his, trying to bring together two disparate kinds of reading, two disparate kinds of knowledge. Aside from the question of possibility or impossibility, I want to note that here as she brings her book to a close, thus putting her writing definitively in the past, becoming no longer a writer but fully an author, she compares herself to Marx. As her writing stops, and the book is done, she compares herself to the writer who exemplified for her the dead author, the author as ghost.

:: :: ::

In my last chapter, I noted how in the foreword to *Tendencies* Sedgwick puts herself in the place of Audre Lorde, a poet who had just died of cancer. Sedgwick, as I put it in that chapter, is identifying with the dead author. Here, at the end of *A Critique of Postcolonial Reason*, Spivak is doing the same thing, identifying with Marx, with the specific figure she has cast as the dead author. I suspect that Sedgwick's and Spivak's shared identification with the dead author might have something to do with the similarly queer temporality of their writing.

Halfway through her last chapter, Spivak states, "My agenda remains an old-fashioned Marxist one" (357). While at other points in the text she seems quite desperate to be up-to-date, here she not only is not apologizing for being "old-fashioned" but sounds defiantly proud of it. In her willingness to be "old-fashioned," Spivak uses the verb "remain," suggesting a certain refusal of movement, a persistence in not chasing after the vanishing present. In the context of the present book, I would connect Spivak's "remaining" to the occurrence of the same verb when Sedgwick says in 2000 that she likes how the printed word "is allowed to remain anachronistic." Spivak's stubborn attachment to the "old-fashioned" sounds a bit like Sedgwick's attachment to the "anachronistic."

I would also want to connect Spivak's characterization of her Marxism as "old-fashioned" to the fact that her book is grappling with the post-Soviet world. In our reading of Sedgwick, we remarked how her appreciation of anachronism was connected to the politics of AIDS, how her experience of gay men dying young and the need to affirm those who had passed, had marked her relation to the temporality of writing. In Spivak's case, the fall of the Soviet Union may function like AIDS does for Sedgwick.

When we looked at the temporality of Sedgwick's writing, we saw how the relation to death interrupted the flow from intended project to actualization. The interruption caused by Owens's death, by Lynch's not dying when expected, and especially by Sedgwick's diagnosis with a life-threatening illness, undid her writing project, radically revised it. We see a similar undoing, radical revision, in Spivak's book, occurring between first completion in the mid-eighties and final revision in the late nineties. What interrupts and derails Spivak's writing is not personal death or illness, but the fall of the Soviet Union and in its wake the much touted "death of Marxism."

After her cancer diagnosis, Sedgwick is writing under the shadow of a personal, quite literal death of the author. While Spivak is also, I would say, shadowed by the author's death as she writes her book, it is not a question here of literal, bodily death that threatens her. Taking Marx as her model at the moment the world proclaims the death of Marxism, she writes in fear of becoming not a literally dead author, but something possibly even worse, an author who while still alive is already a ghost, outmoded, obsolete, not present but stuck in the past.

While Sedgwick identifies with a writer who died just the year before Sedgwick authors her book, Spivak identifies with an author whose literal death occurred long before she was born. What is at stake in Spivak's relation to the dead author is not literal death, but something we might call theoretical death, the threat that Marx's work will be relegated to the past, deemed no longer relevant. Although both Sedgwick and Spivak write in identification with the dead author, Sedgwick is grappling with the effect of literal death while Spivak writes under the shadow of theoretical death, obsolescence.

It is precisely such theoretical death that I found proclaimed in the *New York Times* upon the occasion of Derrida's literal death. Opening the morning paper on October 17, 2004, I read: "With the death on Oct. 8 of the French philosopher Jacques Derrida, the era of big theory came quietly to a close. . . . Deconstruction, Mr. Derrida's primary legacy . . . [t]oday . . . has become a more or less meaningless artifact."[34] While far from the first declaration that theory was dead and ought to be buried, this one used Derrida's literal death to signify a much more total death. I take this *Times* piece as evidence that—however offensive, however indecent it might be—the literal and theoretical deaths of the author are indeed entangled.

The present book has attempted to think the literal and theoretical meanings of the author's death together. In the first chapter a closer look at Barthes's writing made us see that the reader still had feelings for the dead author, but the death in that chapter remained theoretical. It was in the second chapter, as we moved to Derrida's mourning essays, that we began to think about literal, personal death as part of understanding the death of the author. Reading Barthes and Derrida together afforded a conception of the author's death that includes both the theoretical and the personal; it was nonetheless still approached solely from the reader's perspective.

Sedgwick's memorial writing shares with Derrida's a concern with actual, personal death, but in her case the point of view is not so much the reader's but the writer's. Our reading of Sedgwick allowed us to glimpse how the author's death shadows the writer writing, leaving its mark in the writer's engagement with temporality. Following the tracks of that engagement, we came to read Spivak's drama of revising her book, finding in it yet another sort of encounter with the death of the author—this one like Sedgwick's from the writer's point of view, but like Barthes's concerned with theoretical rather than personal death. Taken together, these four chapters aim to revitalize the overly familiar "death of the author" so that we take it as both theoretical and personal, so that we can take a fuller measure of its moving and unsettling effects on readers and writers, on reading and writing.

:: INTRODUCTION

1. The book was Teresa Brennan's *The Transmission of Affect* (Ithaca: Cornell University Press, 2004). My reading of this posthumous book is entitled "Reading Brennan" and can be found in Alice A. Jardine, Shannon Lundeen, and Kelly Oliver, eds., *Living Attention: On Teresa Brennan* (Albany: SUNY Press, 2007), 107–15.

2. Gayatri Chakravorty Spivak, "Reading the *Satanic Verses*," reprinted in *Outside in the Teaching Machine* (Routledge, 1993), 217–19, originally published in *Public Culture* (fall 1989).

3. Michel Foucault, "Qu'est-ce qu'un auteur?" *Bulletin de la Société française de philosophie* 63, no. 3 (July–September, 1969), 73–104. The lecture was delivered on February 22, 1969, to the Société française de philosophie. The lecture is collected in Michel Foucault, *Dits et écrits*, vol. 1 (Paris: Gallimard, 1994), 789–821. An English translation appears in Michel Foucault, *Language, Counter-Memory, Practice*, ed. Donald F. Bouchard (Ithaca: Cornell University Press, 1977), 113–38. Quotations are my translation; the page numbers in parentheses are from *Dits et écrits*, followed by the page from *Language, Counter-Memory, Practice*.

4. 793, 117. In the translation, the paragraph does not end here. The translators (Bouchard and Sherry Simon) have chosen not only to combine this paragraph with the one that follows, but to combine this last sentence of the paragraph with the first of the following paragraph. Thus in the translation, the phrase "death of the author" does not even conclude a sentence, much less a paragraph. The translators do not comment on these decisions of theirs.

5. He is speaking to the prestigious French Society of Philosophy; presiding is Jean Wahl; the last question is posed by Jacques Lacan.

6. 813, not included in the translation. Goldmann inscribes the death of the author in "structuralism," whereas I have filed it under "poststructuralism." Much ink has been spilled on the relation between these two; for my purposes here, let a few remarks suffice. Goldmann names figures belonging to both movements: Lévi-Strauss is the central figure of structuralism; Derrida central to poststructuralism. That he names them together suggests that for Goldmann in 1969 this was not an operative distinction. Barthes had a structuralist phase, followed by a poststructuralist phase; 1969 is located in the midst of the turn from one to the other.

7. "Reading the *Satanic Verses*," 218.

8. Roland Barthes, *Sade, Fourier, Loyola* (Paris: Le Seuil, 1971), 12.

9. Jacques Derrida, *Chaque fois unique, la fin du monde* (Paris: Galilée, 2003), 77.

10. I am very much indebted to Kate Haffey for suggesting this title.

11. Roland Barthes, *Sade, Fourier, Loyola*, 12–13.

12. Eve Kosofsky Sedgwick, *Tendencies* (Durham: Duke University Press, 1993), 256.

13. Stephen Barber and David Clark, "Queer Moments" in *Regarding Sedgwick*, ed. Barber and Clark (Routledge, 2002), 5, quoting from Sedgwick's unpublished "Come As You Are."

14. "This Piercing Bouquet: An Interview with Eve Kosofsky Sedgwick" in *Regarding Sedgwick*, 253.

15. Recent scholarship has in fact claimed anachronism as a queer tem-

porality. See for example, Valerie Rohy, *Anachronism and Its Others: Sexuality, Race, Temporality* (Albany: SUNY Press, 2009).

16. Gayatri Chakravorty Spivak, *A Critique of Postcolonial Reason: Toward a History of the Vanishing Present* (Cambridge: Harvard University Press, 1999), x.

17. 339. Spivak is discussing *Comme des Garçons* as an example of transnationality. Part of her critique of postcolonial reason is her understanding of the current era as not postcolonial but rather transnational.

18. Gayatri Chakravorty Spivak, *The Post-Colonial Critic* (Routledge, 1990), 48.

19. *Sade, Fourier, Loyola*, 11–12.

20. Excerpted from Jane Gallop, "Reading Derrida's Adieu," *differences* 16, no. 3 (fall 2005), 19–21. Italics added. I have made a number of cuts and some other small changes in the text for the sake of clarity and focus.

21. Jacques Derrida, *Adieu à Emmanuel Lévinas* (Paris: Galilée, 1997), 23, translated as Jacques Derrida, *Adieu to Emmanuel Lévinas* (Palo Alto: Stanford University Press, 1999), 9. All translations are modified.

22. Lévinas is himself a thinker of the trace, and it could even be said that Derrida adopts "the trace" from Lévinas. See Robert Bernasconi, "The Trace of Lévinas in Derrida" in *Derrida and Différance*, ed. David Wood and Robert Bernasconi (Warwick: Parousia, 1985), 122–39.

23. Dozens of pages later, Derrida talks about the trace as a "grace" (177, 101). "Reading Derrida's Adieu" connects this idea of the trace as a grace (the saving gift we do not deserve but is generously given us) with the earlier miracle of the trace.

24. Jacques Derrida, *Chaque fois unique, la fin du monde* (Paris: Galilée, 2003), 53.

25. Much of Derrida's early work is involved with exposing the phonocentrism at the heart of philosophy and linguistics. See especially his first book, *Voice and Phenomenon*, and his most influential *Of Grammatology*.

26. Emily Eakin, "The Theory of Everything, R.I.P.," *New York Times*, 17 October 2004, § 4, 12.

1. Seán Burke, *The Death and Return of the Author: Criticism and Subjectivity in Barthes, Foucault and Derrida*, 2d ed. (Edinburgh: Edinburgh University Press, 1998), 19. Further page references will appear parenthetically in the text.

2. Before appearing in French in 1968, "The Death of the Author" in fact appeared in an American literary magazine *Aspen*, nos. 5–6, in 1967.

3. Roland Barthes, "La mort de l'auteur," *Manteia* 5 (1968), 17. English translation "The Death of the Author," in Roland Barthes, *Image-Music-Text*, trans. Stephen Heath (New York: Hill and Wang, 1977), 148. While all translations of Barthes in this chapter are my own, I will also supply page references to a published translation. After the first reference to a text, page numbers will appear in parentheses in the text; the first number refers to the French original, the second to the English translation.

4. Roland Barthes, *Sade, Fourier, Loyola* (Paris: Le Seuil, 1971, collection Points), 12. English translation: *Sade, Fourier, Loyola*, trans. Richard Miller (New York: Hill and Wang, 1976), 8.

5. Roland Barthes, *Le plaisir du texte* (Paris: Le Seuil, 1974, collection Points), 45, emphasis Barthes's. English translation: *The Pleasure of the Text*, trans. Richard Miller (New York: Hill and Wang, 1975), 27.

6. The chapter titles (e.g., "Fetish") do not appear in the text but can be found in the table of contents.

7. "This book is the trace of work done during a two-year seminar (1968 and 1969), held at the Ecole pratique des Hautes Etudes." Roland Barthes, *S/Z* (Paris: Le Seuil, 1970, collection Points), 7; English translation: *S/Z: An Essay*, trans. Richard Miller (New York: Hill and Wang, 1974), vii.

8. Note Burke's use of the word "enliven" in the context of a discussion of the death of the author.

9. Burke wittily connects the capitalizations to the manifesto's exhortation to violence: "the capitalizations prime for decapitation" (26).

10. "What is an Author?" *Bulletin de la Société française de philosophie* 63, no. 3 (July–September 1969). See discussion in the beginning of our Introduction.

11. Unfortunately Richard Miller chose to render "principes de *bio-graphie*" as "*biographical* principles," losing the hyphen that he included in his translation of *S/Z* (211).

12. I am grateful to Seán Burke for reminding me of how important this little-read book is to our understanding of Barthes's relation to the author.

13. Plurality and perversion connect in Barthes via the Freudian notion of polymorphous perverse sexuality, which contrasts with the "unity" of normative adult sexuality.

14. These "*bursts* of memory" may have some connection with Proust's sense of memory; it is a bit later in this same (very long) sentence that Proust shows up.

15. This penultimate paragraph of the preface to *Sade, Fourier, Loyola* is composed of five sentences. The first is a short, simple sentence, and then each succeeding sentence is considerably longer than the one before it.

16. This negative sense of "destiny" is found in Barthes's work as early as his first book, *Le degré zéro de l'écriture*: "The Novel is a Death: it makes life into a destiny" (Paris: Le Seuil, 1971, collection Points), 33.

17. Roland Barthes, *La chambre claire: Note sur la photographie* (Paris: Etoile, Gallimard, Seuil, 1980), 23. English translation: *Camera Lucida: Reflections on Photography*, trans. Richard Howard (New York: Hill and Wang, 1981), 9.

18. 54, 30. We might add "History" to the epic, the stele, etc. as "instructors of destiny" that contrast with the novelistic, the biographeme and, here, the photograph. In *La chambre claire*, Barthes contrasts monuments like the stele to the photograph: "Ancient societies managed so that memory, the substitute of life, would be eternal and that at least the thing which spoke Death would be itself immortal: that was the Monument. But in making the (mortal) Photograph the witness . . . of 'what has been,' modern society has renounced the Monument" (146, 93).

19. We might even want to connect this to the use of "friendship" as euphemism for queer sexual relations, which I touch on in chapter 3, in my reading of Sedgwick's memorial for Craig Owens.

20. Barthes uses the verb *essaimer* which literally means "swarm," like bees, but figuratively means to scatter, to disperse, drawing upon the fact that swarming involves leaving the hive. Unfortunately, Miller in his translation renders this as "hangs together," losing the resonance with the next paragraph's "dispersion."

21. This "other" or "Other" who enters our lives, who comes to live with us, calls to mind Emmanuel Lévinas's ethics of hospitality to the other in *Totalité et infini*. While it would, I think, be fruitful to articulate Barthes's relation to the author with Lévinas's sense of the other, that is a large undertaking, unfortunately beyond our focus here.

22. In fact he uses it three times if we also count its occurrence at the very beginning of the next paragraph: "The pleasure of the Text also includes the friendly return of the author."

23. 45, 27. The "/" marks the paragraph break.

24. *The Pleasure of the Text* in fact proposes an erotics of what is "in the middle": "In perversion . . . it is intermittence . . . which is erotic: that of the skin scintillating between two pieces (pants and sweater), between two edges (open shirt, glove, and sleeve); it is this very scintillation which seduces, or rather: the staging of an appearance-disappearance" (19, 9–10). This, I would say, is the mode in which, according to Barthes, the author appears in the text: we catch flickering glimpses of the author. It may be precisely the author's position "in the middle" of the text that elicits Barthes's desire.

25. In *The Pleasure of the Text*, Barthes actually speaks of the perversity of "but" desire: "Many readings are perverse, implying a split. Just as the child knows that his mother has no penis and yet at the same time believes she has one (an economy whose profitability Freud has shown), so the reader can keep saying: *I know of course that these are only words, but all the same . . .*" (76, 47, ellipsis Barthes's). *I know of course, but all the same*: this is the structure of Barthes's desire for the author. This particular structure is not just generally perverse but specifically fetishistic, and, as I noted earlier, the two-paragraph chapter/fragment that we are here reading oh so closely, this chapter/fragment in which he announces his desire for the author, is entitled "Fetish."

26. D. A. Miller, *Bringing Out Roland Barthes* (Berkeley: University of

California Press, 1992), 7, emphasis added. Miller's fantasy is a reader's fantasy of bodily contact with a dead author: "What I most seek now . . . is the opportunity . . . for fashioning . . . an intimacy with the writer whom . . . I otherwise can't touch" (ibid.). This possibility of touching recalls Barthes's fantasy in *Sade, Fourier, Loyola*; just as the "intimacy" reminds me of the "living with the author" in the same text.

27. Chapter 3 of this book will return us to the year 1992, and to gay men dying of AIDS. The connections between this first chapter (on Barthes) and the third chapter (on Sedgwick) begin to sketch out a queer ethics of reading death, an insistence on the erotics of reading the dead. As Michael Moon (quoted in chapter 3) puts it: "Allowing our sex radicalism to pervade our mourning practices . . . to conduct our mourning and grieving . . . as an indispensable part of . . . exploring 'perverse' . . . desire" (unpublished manuscript, quoted in *Tendencies*, 258). The congruences between my first and third chapters point toward another book I might have written, a book more centered in queer sex radicalism, less centered in the temporality of reading and writing.

Chapter 2 :: THE ETHICS OF INDECENCY

1. Jacques Derrida, "Les morts de Roland Barthes," *Poétique* 47 (September 1981).

2. "Les morts de Roland Barthes" in Jacques Derrida, *Chaque fois unique, la fin du monde* (Paris: Galilée, 2003), 77, emphasis Derrida's. Translated as "The Deaths of Roland Barthes" in Jacques Derrida, *The Work of Mourning* (Chicago: University of Chicago Press, 2001), 49–50, translation modified. Further page references will appear in the text in parentheses: the first number will refer to the French edition; the second number to the English edition, e.g. (77, 49–50); I will regularly modify the published translation.

3. Derrida readily treats his living friends as authors, often and pleasurably writing readings of their texts. What he cannot bear is to treat his dead friends as authors—or is it to treat his friends as dead authors?

4. Roland Barthes, *Sade, Fourier, Loyola*, 12.

5. For readers for whom this allusion is too quick, let me just say that Derrida is known for having shown that there is no pure origin, for having reversed the relation between origin and secondary version, and for having shown difference already at work in whatever we might take to be an origin. So an original which is already a translation could be seen to exemplify the Derridian deconstruction of origins.

6. Jacques Derrida, *Adieu à Emmanuel Lévinas* (Paris: Galilée, 1997), 8, translation mine. This passage appears (somewhat differently translated) in the English translation, *Adieu to Emmanuel Lévinas* (Palo Alto: Stanford University Press, 1999), ix.

7. Let me note that precipitation and the too fast are criticized in the pieces on Althusser (150), Marin (204), and Blanchot (327), among others.

8. While it is true that the reader of *Adieu* does not know who wrote these words, in the English translation of *Adieu* this statement is signed with the initials J. D. and—rather than "we would never have dared"—is translated "I would never have dared."

9. To take the initiative is to make the first move; to initiate is to originate. There is a connection here to origins: what Derrida "would never dare" do here is originate, never dare be at the origin. There is something intolerable, indecent, obscene about being at the origin here, which leads me to wonder about the impetus of Derrida's lifelong deconstruction of origins.

10. *Critical Inquiry* 23, no. 1 (autumn 1996) and *Philosophy Today* 40, no. 3 (fall 1996).

11. The latter do appear on the cover and the title page, in a position supplementary to the author. The cover says, in letters much smaller than the author's name, "Presented by Pascale-Anne Brault and Michael Naas"; the title page has "Texts presented by Pascale-Anne Brault and Michael Naas." Let us note that all these formal appearances put Brault first, Naas second, whereas Derrida's comment in the foreword reverses the order.

12. Brault's and Naas's introductory essay, "To Reckon with the Dead: Jacques Derrida's Politics of Mourning," was originally published in the American edition; the authors themselves translated it into French for the French edition. When quoting from their text, I will quote from

the English version, but for the sake of consistency (and to avoid confusion) I will put the French page numbers first, followed by the English page numbers, in the parenthetical references.

13. Although I will not be spending a lot of time on Derrida's memorial for Kofman, there are two things I must note: (1) of the 16 friends/authors memorialized in the volume, Kofman is the only woman; (2) more hauntingly, *Chaque fois unique* appears in a book series edited by four people—Derrida, Philippe Lacoue-Labarthe, Jean-Luc Nancy, and Sarah Kofman. Her name is thus listed on the 2003 book as currently editing the series despite the fact that she died in 1994.

14. I would connect the liveness of the *parole* here, this gesture of letting the dead friend speak, with Derrida's marveling in *Adieu* at how, after his death, "Lévinas speaks to us"—a subject I discuss above in my introduction.

15. Before I say more about this passage from Brault and Naas, I need to confess that I keep having the urge to "modify the translation" of their text by changing "citation" to "quotation," but then I recall that they composed their text in English. Whenever they write "citation," I always wish they had written "quotation"; I feel as if they are mistranslating from the French *citation*. I imagine that in this they are influenced by the term "citationality," often used in Derridian theories.

16. The question of responsibility in this book involves Brault and Naas in another way. In the preface to the French edition, Derrida says, "I believed I should accept this proposition: that . . . Michael Naas and Pascale-Anne Brault . . . *take responsibility* for an American edition" (10, emphasis added). He goes on to say that the book "is their book," that they are the "true authors." Authorship is connected to taking responsibility. Calling Naas and Brault "the true authors," giving them the responsibility, seems to be a way of avoiding indecency. For a moment, it seems as if Derrida is trying to avoid responsibility for the indecency of *The Work of Mourning*. Responsibility, and authorship, however, remain complex. He might call them the "true authors," but it is his name on the cover of the book, and he chooses to write a foreword. The very foreword in which he calls them the "true authors" can also be seen as an act of speaking as the author, of taking responsibility for this book. Given his sense of the indecency of the book, perhaps what he wants is not so much to avoid responsibility as to share responsibility.

17. One sign of this is the frequent appearance of the word "moment" (and similar words) in the passages I quote from Derrida here.

18. The image here of cutting the text reminds me of Derrida's discussion of the Rembrandt painting in his essay on Kofman. In the painting, called *The Anatomy Lesson*, the corpse is literally being cut into. (In fact the instrument used by the doctors in the Rembrandt painting is the scissors, the very instrument of *découpage*.) If the substitution "of the corpus for the corpse appears to be the only chance the dead have left," as Brault and Naas suggest following Derrida's reading of Kofman, it seems ironic that as a result of this substitution, the text will find itself carved up, cut into, like the corpse it replaces. "The Anatomy Lesson" becomes an emblem for the violence of reading the dead author's text.

19. I might just mention that, decades ago, I happened to write about Blanchot's memorial for Bataille in a little article I called "Reading Friends' Corpses" (*MLN*, 95, no. 4 (1980), 1017–22). I'm still wondering about the relation of my long-ago essay to the present work.

20. This is what Derrida has called "iterability." For Derrida, the repetition of "iterability" always includes the possibility of alteration, mutation. This mutability is, I would imagine, particularly troubling in the context of this genre, where the poignancy of the occasion makes iterability indecent.

21. Derrida's phrasing here is hard to translate. The French reads: *je souffre beaucoup de devoir, faute de temps, ne pas tout lire*. Brault and Naas translate: "I suffer so much at not being able, for lack of time, to read everything." The problem is translating the word *devoir* which can mean "duty" and here as a verb means something like "have to," leading to the awkward "have to not read everything," a phrase made even more difficult by the phrase "for lack of time" that interrupts it. With its sense of duty, the word *devoir* seems particularly resonant in the context of a consideration of the ethics of quotation. Boris Belay's translation in *The Work of Mourning* does not translate *devoir*; I chose to translate it by "necessity," although I am not satisfied with this translation.

22. Thinking about the horror of isolation or abandonment suggests perhaps why Derrida might want to share authorship of this book with two "friends" (Naas and Brault). In the context of this work of mourn-

ing, there is a particular violence or indecency associated with leaving the author alone that contrasts with some togetherness with friends.

23. There is a memorial to de Man in *Chaque fois unique*, not the one I am about to quote but a shorter one, delivered two months earlier.

24. Jacques Derrida, *Mémoires pour Paul de Man* (Paris: Galilée, 1988), 64, my translation. An English translation of this lecture by Jonathan Culler was published in *Memoires for Paul de Man* (New York: Columbia University Press, 1986), 50–51. We might note that here too the English translation was published before the French edition.

25. Brault's and Naas's use of "cite" where I would use "quote" slightly obscures the similarity of these two phrases. In their 2001 French translation of their introduction, they revise this sentence, changing it to "Derrida thus cites and interrupts the word of the other."

26. I note the dialogism here in part because of a question Dale Bauer asked me at a lecture I gave on the present book project at Champaign-Urbana in October 2005.

27. There seems to be, actually on either side of the "impossible choice," a risk of pluralizing death, a reduplication of death: on the one hand, "send[ing] death back to death"; on the other, "adding death to death."

28. This reminds me of Sedgwick's saying—when talking about the memorial genre—that what most upset her in the AIDS quilt was reading *in the quilt* "HE HATED THE QUILT" in *Tendencies* (Durham: Duke University Press), 265.

Part II :: IF I WERE A WRITER AND DEAD

1. Roland Barthes, *Sade, Fourier, Loyola*, 12–13; translation, 8; see chapter 1 above, 29–53.

Chapter 3 :: THE QUEER TEMPORALITY OF WRITING

1. Derrida's mourning essays date from 1981 to 2003. 1990 and 1991 are not only the approximate midpoint of this range but are the most over-represented years in the collection: 1990 and 1991 each saw Derrida

write three memorials. Only one other year (1995) has more than one memorial.

2. There are of course hints in Derrida too that indecency has to do with timing.

3. The title's "T" presumably refers to these "T-shirts," the all-caps "QUEER" quoting from the shirts. Eve Kosofsky Sedgwick, *Tendencies* (Durham: Duke University Press, 1993), xi. Further references will appear (parenthetically) in the text.

4. Stephen M. Barber and David L. Clark, "Queer Moments: The Performative Temporalities of Eve Kosofsky Sedgwick" in Barber and Clark, eds., *Regarding Sedgwick: Essays on Queer Culture and Critical Theory* (New York: Routledge, 2002), 2, emphasis in the original.

5. See, for example, *Queer Temporalities*. Special Issue of GLQ: *A Journal of Gay and Lesbian Studies* 13, nos. 2–3 (2007). A prior version of the present chapter—forthcoming in the collection *Queer Times, Queer Becomings*, edited by Ellen McCallum and Mikko Tuhkanen—was written to contribute to this inquiry.

6. Eve Kosofsky Sedgwick, *Fat Art, Thin Art* (Durham: Duke University Press, 1994), 11. Barber and Clark quote only the second stanza.

7. "The Navajo Rug," ibid., 12.

8. "Joy. He's himself today! He knows me!" ibid., 9. Barber and Clark attribute this title to the poem they use as epigraph. That poem, appearing two pages later in *Fat Art* has no title and is identified only by its first line: "Guys who are 35 last year are 70 this year."

9. "Performative (San Francisco)," ibid., 18.

10. I've quoted only two of these sentences; sentences not quoted mention the upcoming inauguration of a president who claims to support gay rights, "massive participation" in the pride march "for the first time" by African Americans and Latinos, organizing around the right to be soldiers, etc.

11. In the parenthesis we also find the phrase "long moment of a deathly silence," which resonates with "the long moment of no more" in one of the gay writers dying with AIDS poems.

12. Thinking Sedgwick and Barthes together, we might want to remark, among other things, their quite similarly casual redeployments of Freudian theory.

13. "Quasi" because of Sedgwick's use of "love" which Freud is unlikely to use with the discourse of "part-objects." For an understanding of the Freudian part-object, see Freud's *Three Essays on a Theory of Sexuality*, and Jean Laplanche's *Life and Death in Psychoanalysis*, chap. 5. After hearing a draft of my chapter, Lauren Berlant suggested that "part-objects" is Kleinian, not Freudian, that it represents Sedgwick's engagement with the works of Melanie Klein.

14. While it is grammatically unclear whether friendship is the only euphemism here—or whether "love at a distance" and "reading and writing" constitute alternative euphemisms—I am reading this passage as if "friendship" were the only euphemism because of the term's history as euphemism for queer relations, a history not shared by the two alternatives that follow. How often "friendship" is precisely the euphemism to cover over queer sexual relations!

15. Roland Barthes, *Sade, Fourier, Loyola*, 12.

16. Ibid.

17. Eve Kosofsky Sedgwick, *Between Men: English Literature and Male Homosocial Desire* (New York: Columbia University Press, 1992), viii–ix.

18. "In some cryptic but very provocative paragraphs in his essay 'Outlaws: Gay Men in Feminism,' Craig Owens suggests. . . ." "Tales of the Avunculate: Queer Tutelage in *The Importance of Being Earnest*," in *Tendencies*, 61–62, 72.

19. I have to say that, currently revising this chapter for the third time, as I work on this section I find myself nearly overcome by my anxiety that it will never be finished.

20. I do love this essay, think it important and valuable, which makes me grateful she was able to finish it, and makes me care more about her difficulties writing it, while still feeling uncomfortable about how she made those difficulties the topic of her memorial.

21. Craig Owens, "Outlaws: Gay Men in Feminism" in *Beyond Recogni-*

tion: *Representation, Power, and Culture* (Berkeley: University of California Press, 1992), 226–28.

22. The subtitle of "Tales of Avunculate" is "Queer Tutelage in *The Importance of Being Earnest.*" "Queer Tutelage" is also the title of this section of *Tendencies*, the one that ends with the "Memorial to Craig Owens." The authorizing position that both Owens and Lynch play in regard to this essay in fact exemplifies what Sedgwick calls "queer tutelage."

23. Michael Moon, "Memorial Rags, Memorial Rages," quoted by Sedgwick in "White Glasses," 258. Moon is another gay writer friend who plays an important role in *Tendencies*. The penultimate essay in the collection, appearing just before "White Glasses," is in fact coauthored by Sedgwick and Moon.

24. *American Heritage Dictionary* (Boston: Houghton Mifflin, 1969), 1196, emphasis added.

25. This image of being "surprised from behind" might be connected to Sedgwick's avowed pleasure in being taken from behind, a pleasure she confesses in an essay collected in *Tendencies*, "A Poem is Being Written."

26. As we saw in the last chapter, memorials generically have such a double address—to the deceased and to the mourners.

27. This seemingly upbeat sentence is, however, interrupted by two parenthetical remarks. The first of these—"I thought I could"—occasions yet another repetition of "I thought." While the main line of the sentence treats not being able to address Lynch as a necessity ("have to"), the parenthetical construes it as an opportunity ("could"). I found myself reading this "I thought I could" over and over in disbelief, looking for some way to understand it other than as an expression of disappointment (as in, I thought I could . . . but now I can't). It seems to mark how Michael's not dying is a disconcerting surprise, not just happy but unsettling, undermining her plans for this obituary.

28. http://education.yahoo.com/reference/dictionary/entry/yikes.

29. Barber and Clark use the plural "temporalities" in their subtitle while my title uses the singular "temporality." In the text they use both plural and singular. The phrase I borrow from them for my title, "queer temporality," occurs in the singular in their text.

30. Barber and Clark, "Queer Moments," 5, quoting from Sedgwick's unpublished "Come As You Are."

31. "This Piercing Bouquet: An Interview with Eve Kosofsky Sedgwick" in *Regarding Sedgwick*, 253.

Chapter 4 :: THE PERSISTENT AND VANISHING PRESENT

1. Barber and Clark, "Queer Moments," 2.

2. Spivak, *Outside in the Teaching Machine* (New York: Routledge, 1993), 156.

3. "Strategy, Identity, Writing," first published in *Melbourne Journal of Politics* 18 (1986/87), collected in Gayatri Spivak, *The Post-Colonial Critic: Interviews, Strategies, Dialogues*, ed. Sarah Harasym (New York: Routledge, 1990), 48. While the interviewers are named in the headnote (John Hutnyk, Scott McQuire, and Nikos Papastergiadis), the text does not distinguish their questions, attributing all questions to "MJP" (*Melbourne Journal of Politics*).

4. *Webster's Third New International Dictionary* (Springfield, Mass.: Merriam-Webster, 1986), 1684. Interestingly, it turns out that the etymology of "perpetrate" is from the Latin "perform in the capacity of a father," from *pater (American Heritage Dictionary of the English Language*, 977).

5. Gayatri Chakravorty Spivak, *In Other Worlds* (New York: Routledge, 2006), ii.

6. Like *In Other Worlds*, *Outside in the Teaching Machine* is a collection of essays.

7. Thinking about her theoretical relation to books, I would just note that the first chapter of the book by Derrida that Spivak translated in the 1970s (*Of Grammatology*) is entitled "The End of the Book and the Beginning of Writing."

8. Gayatri Chakravorty Spivak, *A Critique of Postcolonial Reason: Toward a History of the Vanishing Present* (Cambridge: Harvard University Press, 1999), 153.

9. In a 1985 interview, also included in *The Post-Colonial Critic*, Spivak gives a chapter breakdown of the manuscript entitled "Master Discourse — Native Informant: Deconstruction in the Service of Reading." My sense of the contents of the manuscript she discusses in the interview with MJP a year later comes from this 1985 "chapter breakdown" ("The *Intervention* Interview," *The Post-Colonial Critic*, 132).

10. Spivak's most recent book, *Other Asias* (Blackwell, 2008), continues the practice of such late-breaking bulletin footnotes (or in this case, endnotes). A number of notes refer to what she read in the morning's *New York Times*; one of the latest drafted notes opens: "And this just in" (314 n. 75).

11. "Subaltern Studies: Deconstructing Historiography" in *In Other Worlds*, 285.

12. Spivak gets "historical sense" and the contrast between it and traditional history from Michel Foucault, "Nietzsche, Genealogy, History" in *Language, Counter-Memory, Practice*, ed. Donald Bouchard (Ithaca: Cornell University Press, 1977).

13. Spivak gets "history of the present" from Michel Foucault, *Discipline and Punish*, trans. Alan Sheridan (New York: Pantheon, 1977).

14. Spivak actually says "1995 Atlanta Olympics," *Postcolonial Reason*, 367 n. 76, but the Atlanta Olympics were in 1996.

15. See chapter 3, 87–114, quoting from "This Piercing Bouquet: An Interview with Eve Kosofsky Sedgwick" in *Regarding Sedgwick*, 253.

16. It might be relevant that both are speaking on the cusp of a new millennium.

17. The idea of the footnotes as "moving" might refer to the way they keep changing, to her persistent revision of these notes.

18. "More on Power/Knowledge" (originally published in 1992), collected in Gayatri Chakravorty Spivak, *Outside in the Teaching Machine*, 30–31. She gets the phrase from Michel Foucault, *La volonté de savoir* (Paris: Gallimard, 1976), 122.

19. Catachrestic concept-metaphor is her way of explaining how Derrida's writing works (for example, *différance, supplément, pharmakon*

are catachrestic concept-metaphors). Finding a catachrestic concept-metaphor in Foucault seems to be part of the process of bringing him closer to Derrida, in this 1992 essay whose explicit project is "Reading Foucault and Derrida Together."

20. The sense of insecurity in "teetering" may be amplified by characterizing herself here as "one woman": the "one" emphasizing her solitude and also a certain limitation (as in how much can *one* woman do?), the reference to her gender as she is teetering making her perhaps a bit of a damsel in distress.

21. And she says "charts," which also suggests a certain mastery of the landscape.

22. The alliterative "practitioner's progress" might even allude to John Bunyan's canonical *Pilgrim's Progress*.

23. I do not quote the fifth and final sentence of the note where Spivak wonders if her insubordinate footnotes might not be a "vulgar version" of what Derrida undertook "with intent" in "Border Lines" and "Circumfessions." While it might be possible to understand Spivak's footnotes as working like Derrida's, I would want to emphasize that even as she makes the comparison, she makes it clear that he was doing this intentionally while she was not. Although we might be able to justify Spivak's out-of-control footnotes as Derridian, this note makes it clear that she was not intending to follow that model.

24. See chapter 3, 87–114, quoting from *Between Men* (1992), viii–ix.

25. The verb "reports" fits with the idea of the newscaster's bulletin; it is the same verb that Spivak uses in the footnote we looked at from the middle of the last chapter—"as the morning news reports" (339).

26. I have left the one word "invagination" out of this quotation. "Invagination" is a word Spivak takes from Derrida and uses to represent the effect of her updating footnotes, the way they take over and undermine the book. It would be really interesting to consider the gender politics of this word as Spivak takes it up from Derrida, but I will not do that here, instead remaining with my topic of her encounter with temporality. I will just say that using the word "invagination" is part of the attempt to justify her insubordinate footnotes as Derridian.

27. Spivak, "Introduction to the Routledge Classics Edition," *In Other Worlds*, x–xi. And in a book published the following year she says: "My work on socialist ethics has been thirty-one years in the making. I still do not know if I can write it as the world changes—but let me end with promise of future work" (*Other Asias*, 11).

28. Given the insistence of the image of uncertain footing in Spivak's figuration of the author's dilemma, I am struck by some lines of poetry by Farhad Mazhar that Spivak translates from Bengali and quotes in a long, narrative footnote in the middle of the last chapter of *Postcolonial Reason*: "I am slipping. My foot is losing its hold./ I am taking down with my heel the problems of my footing" (362, from Mazhar, *Ashomoyer Noteboi* [Dhaka: Protipokkho, 1994], 42).

29. See Spivak, "Ghostwriting," *Diacritics* 25, no. 2 (1995), 65–84, and Derrida, *Specters of Marx*, trans. Peggy Kamuf (New York: Routledge, 1994).

30. Looking at her wording, it seems that Spivak too knows that Barthes's relation to the author is more complex than the polemical and oft-cited "closing passage" of "The Death of the Author" (98).

31. See chapter 1 of the present book, 29–53, quoting from Barthes, *Sade, Fourier, Loyola*, 12.

32. We recognize the verb for her persistence in the "keep" of "keep pushing away."

33. At the end of the penultimate sentence about whether the two different sorts of texts can be stitched together, we find a footnote (the last of the book) that reads: "It must be acknowledged that Derrida attempted such a stitching in *Glas*. . . . But that, too, is only European-focus." Derrida also functions as a model for Spivak the author. In what I quote here, the "too" refers to what she is about to say about Marx. Derrida too, in addition to Marx, "is only European-focus." Derrida gets the last footnote; Marx gets the last sentence in the text.

34. Eakin, "The Theory of Everything, R.I.P."; see discussion in my introduction, 1–26.

::

WORKS CITED

::

Barber, Stephen M., and David L. Clark. "Queer Moments: The Performative Temporalities of Eve Kosofsky Sedgwick." In *Regarding Sedgwick: Essays on Queer Culture and Critical Theory*, ed. Stephen M. Barber and David L. Clark, 1–54. New York: Routledge, 2002.

Barber, Stephen M., and David L. Clark, eds. *Regarding Sedgwick: Essays on Queer Culture and Critical Theory*. New York: Routledge, 2002.

Barthes, Roland. *La chambre claire: Note sur la photographie*. Paris: Etoile, Gallimard, Le Seuil, 1980.

———. *Camera Lucida: Reflections on Photography*. Trans. Richard Howard. New York: Hill and Wang, 1981.

———. *Le degré zéro de l'écriture*. Paris: Le Seuil, 1971, collection Points.

———. *Image-Music-Text*. Trans. Stephen Heath. New York: Hill and Wang, 1977.

———. "La mort de l'auteur." *Manteia* 5 (1968).

———. "The Death of the Author." In *Image-Music-Text*. Trans. Stephen Heath. New York: Hill and Wang, 1977. 142–48.

———. *Le plaisir du texte*. Paris: Le Seuil, 1974, collection Points.

———. *The Pleasure of the Text*. Trans. Richard Miller. New York: Hill and Wang, 1975.

———. *Sade, Fourier, Loyola*. Paris: Le Seuil, 1971.

———. *Sade, Fourier, Loyola*. Trans. Richard Miller. New York: Hill and
Wang, 1976.

———. *S/Z*. Paris: Le Seuil, 1970, collection Points.

———. *S/Z: An Essay*. Trans. Richard Miller. New York: Hill and
Wang, 1974.

Bernasconi, Robert. "The Trace of Lévinas in Derrida." In *Derrida and
Différance*, ed. David Wood and Robert Bernasconi, 122–39. Warwick:
Parousia, 1985.

Brennan, Teresa. *The Transmission of Affect*. Ithaca: Cornell University
Press, 2004.

Burke, Seán. *The Death and Return of the Author: Criticism and Subjectivity
in Barthes, Foucault and Derrida*. 2d ed. Edinburgh: Edinburgh University
Press, 1998.

Derrida, Jacques. *Adieu à Emmanuel Lévinas*. Paris: Galilée, 1997.

———. *Adieu to Emmanuel Lévinas*. Trans. Pascale-Anne Brault and
Michael Naas. Palo Alto: Stanford University Press, 1999.

———. *Chaque fois unique, la fin du monde*. Paris: Galilée, 2003.

———. *The Work of Mourning*. Chicago: University of Chicago Press,
2001.

———. *Mémoires pour Paul de Man*. Paris: Galilée, 1988.

———. *Memoires for Paul de Man*. New York: Columbia University Press,
1986.

———. "Les morts de Roland Barthes." *Poétique* 47 (September 1981),
269–92.

———. "The Deaths of Roland Barthes." In *The Work of Mourning*,
Jacques Derrida, 31–68. Chicago: University of Chicago Press,
2001.

———. *Of Grammatology*. Trans. Gayatri Chakravorty Spivak. Baltimore: Johns Hopkins University Press, 1998.

———. *Specters of Marx*. Trans. Peggy Kamuf. New York: Routledge,
1994.

———. *La voix et le phénomène*. Paris: Presses Universitaires de France,
1967.

———. *Speech and Phenomena*. Evanston: Northwestern University
Press, 1973.

Eakin, Emily. "The Theory of Everything, R.I.P.," *New York Times*, 17 October 2004, § 4, 12.

Foucault, Michel. *Discipline and Punish*. Trans. Alan Sheridan. New York: Pantheon, 1977.

———. *Language, Counter-Memory, Practice*, ed. Donald F. Bouchard. Ithaca: Cornell University Press, 1977.

———. "Nietzsche, Genealogy, History." In *Language, Counter-Memory, Practice*, ed. Donald Bouchard, 139–64. Ithaca: Cornell University Press, 1977.

———. "Qu'est-ce qu'un auteur?" *Bulletin de la Société française de philosophie* 63, no. 3 (July–September, 1969): 73–104.

———. *La volonté de savoir*. Paris: Gallimard, 1976.

Freeman, Elizabeth, ed. *Queer Temporalities*. Special Issue of GLQ: *A Journal of Gay and Lesbian Studies* 13, nos. 2–3 (2007).

Freud, Sigmund. *Three Essays on a Theory of Sexuality*. Trans. James Strachey. New York: Basic Books, 2000.

Gallop, Jane. "Reading Brennan." In *Living Attention: On Teresa Brennan*, ed. Alice A. Jardine, Shannon Lundeen, and Kelly Oliver, 107–15. Albany: SUNY Press, 2007.

———. "Reading Derrida's Adieu." *differences* 16, no. 3 (fall 2005): 19–21.

———. "Reading Friends' Corpses." *MLN* 95, no. 4 (1980): 1017–22.

Laplanche, Jean. *Life and Death in Psychoanalysis*. Trans. Jeffrey Mehlman. Baltimore: Johns Hopkins University Press, 1976.

Lévinas, Emmanuel. *Totalité et Infini*. Paris: Livre de Poche, 1990.

Mazhar, Farhad. *Ashomoyer Noteboi*. Dhaka: Protipokkho, 1994.

McCallum, Ellen, and Mikko Tuhkanen, eds. *Queer Times, Queer Becomings*. Albany: SUNY Press, forthcoming.

Miller, D. A. *Bringing Out Roland Barthes*. Berkeley: University of California Press, 1992.

Moon, Michael. "Memorial Rags, Memorial Rages." Unpublished manuscript.

Owens, Craig. "Outlaws: Gay Men in Feminism." In *Beyond Recognition: Representation, Power, and Culture*, 226–28. Berkeley: University of California Press, 1992.

Rohy, Valerie. *Anachronism and Its Others: Sexuality, Race, Temporality*. Albany: SUNY Press, 2009.

Sedgwick, Eve Kosofsky. *Between Men: English Literature and Male Homosocial Desire*. New York: Columbia University Press, 1992.
———. "Come As You Are." Unpublished manuscript.
———. *Fat Art, Thin Art*. Durham: Duke University Press, 1994.
———. *Tendencies*. Durham: Duke University Press, 1993.
———. "This Piercing Bouquet: An Interview with Eve Kosofsky Sedgwick." In *Regarding Sedgwick: Essays on Queer Culture and Critical Theory*, ed. Stephen M. Barber and David L. Clark, 243–62. New York: Routledge, 2002.

Spivak, Gayatri Chakravorty. *A Critique of Postcolonial Reason: Toward a History of the Vanishing Present*. Cambridge: Harvard University Press, 1999.
———. "Ghostwriting." *Diacritics* 25, no. 2 (1995): 65–84.
———. *In Other Worlds*. New York: Routledge, 2006.
———. *Other Asias*. Oxford: Blackwell, 2008.
———. *Outside in the Teaching Machine*. New York: Routledge, 1993.
———. *The Post-Colonial Critic: Interviews, Strategies, Dialogues*. Ed. Sarah Harasym. New York: Routledge, 1990.
———. "Reading the *Satanic Verses*." In *Outside in the Teaching Machine*, 217–19. New York: Routledge, 1993.

AIDS: death and, 88, 91–92, 95, 100–101, 110–13, 151n27; poems about, 90, 105, 156n11; politics of, 95, 142; queerness and, 11, 52, 88, 91; quilt memorial for, 155n28

Althusser, Louis, 4, 67, 69–71, 75, 77

Anachronism, 13–15, 117, 119, 124, 127–28, 142, 146n15; of printed word, 112–14

Authority, 16, 130, 137

Balzac, Honoré de, 32, 33

Barber, Stephen, 9, 12, 89–92, 106, 112, 115–16, 124

Barthes, Roland, 51–53; autobiography of, 45, 80–81; "biography" by, 35–37, 39, 41, 45, 48; *Camera Lucida*, 45, 46, 56; "The Death of the Author,"

2–8, 29–42, 46; Derrida and, 7–8, 18, 55–60, 69–70, 79–83, 143–44; erotics of, 59, 61, 82, 93; *The Pleasure of the Text*, 5, 30–31, 37–40, 49–50, 93–94, 150nn24–25; *Sade, Fourier, Loyola*, 5–6, 9, 30–31, 35–49, 87–88; Sedgwick and, 88, 92–93; Spivak and, 16, 137–38, 162n30; *S/Z*, 32–37, 39; *Writing Degree Zero*, 149n16

Bataille, Georges, 72, 73

Baudelaire, Charles, 121

Between Men (Sedgwick), 94, 133

Biographeme, 45, 48, 49

"Bio-graphy," 35–37, 39, 41, 45, 48

Blanchot, Maurice, 71–73

Brault, Pascale-Anne, 62–70, 75–81, 152n12, 153n16

Brennan, Teresa, 145n1

Buddhism, 109

Bunyan, John, 161n22
Burke, Seán, 5, 29–32, 40, 45

Cancer, 12, 17, 107–10, 141
Chaque fois unique, la fin du monde
(Derrida), 59–82, 88, 155n1
Clark, David, 9, 12, 89–92, 106,
112, 115–16, 124
Co-existence, 49–50, 138
Comme des Garçons (corpora-
tion), 14, 122–23, 147n17
Complicity, 16, 137
Corpse/corpus, 66–67, 154n18
Criticism, 3, 34, 36–37, 58, 106;
ethical form of, 19
Critique of Postcolonial Reason, A
(Spivak), 14–17, 118–41
Cultural studies, transnational,
128–30, 132, 134, 140

Dates, insistence on, 103, 111
Death and Return of the Author, The
(Burke), 5, 29–32, 40
"Death of the Author, The"
(Barthes), 2–8, 29–42, 46
Deconstruction, 23, 117–18, 121–
22, 143, 152n5, 152n9
Deicide/parricide, 16, 137
Deleuze, Gilles, 78
De Man, Paul, 77–80, 82,
155nn23–24
Derrida, Jacques, 4; *Adieu à Em-
manuel Lévinas*, 19–24, 61–62;
Althusser and, 67, 69–71, 75,
77; Barthes and, 7–8, 18, 55–59,
69–70, 79–83, 143–44; *Chaque
fois unique, la fin du monde*, 59–
82, 88, 155n1; "The Deaths of

Roland Barthes," 55–60; ethics
of close reading and, 19–20,
24–25; Lyotard and, 73–79,
97; *Mémoires pour Paul de Man*,
78–79, 155n24; memorial for,
19–23; obituary for, 23–24,
143; Riddel and, 68, 71, 75,
77; Sedgwick and, 87–88,
144; *Specters of Marx*, 137,
162n29; Spivak and, 159n7,
160n19, 161n23; *The Work of
Mourning*, 6–9, 64–65, 73–82,
97, 152n12
Desire, 96; for the author, 5, 22,
31, 38, 53, 150n25; for the dead,
11–12, 101; perversity of, 5, 11,
88, 93, 101; queer, 94; as speech,
77–78; stigmatized, 11–12, 101
Destiny, 40–48, 149n16, 149n18
Dialectic, 42–43, 52
Dixon, Melvin, 91, 92, 110

Engagement: ethics of, 78; with
temporality, 18, 144
Erotics, 6, 86, 150n24, 151n27; of
Barthes, 59, 61, 82, 93; the body
and, 37–38, 40, 47. *See also*
Corpse/corpus
Ethics: of the "and yet," 72–75,
82; of close reading, 19–20,
23–24; of Derrida, 7, 59, 78;
of dialogue, 79; of hospitality,
21, 25, 150n21; of indecency,
7, 24, 66–67, 71, 88; of infidelity, 81–82; as queer, 11,
151n27; of quotation, 70–71,
74, 76, 154n21; socialist, 136,
162n27

Fetish, 31, 148n6, 150n25

Fidelity/infidelity, 55–56, 77–82

Figure: figuration and, 37–38; novelistic, 35–36. *See also* Ghosts

Footnotes, 14; as insubordinate, 161n23, 161n26; "meta," 126, 127; narrative, 125–35, 160n10, 160n17, 162n28

Foucault, Michel: Spivak and, 123, 129, 160n18, 160nn12–13; "What Is an Author?," 2–4, 34, 42, 46

Fragility, 11, 97, 100

France, 2, 29, 60–61

Friends/friendship, 6, 68, 93, 149n19, 157n14; allowing speech by dead, 75–76, 80, 153n14; authors as, 58, 63–64, 67, 71–72, 97, 151n3; departed, 7, 56, 117; indecency and, 82, 87

Gaze, 21; of shock and mourning, 12, 108–9

Genet, Jean, 36–39

Genre, 25, 41, 77, 80, 93, 154n20; of memorial essay, 6–10, 20, 55, 58, 71–73, 82–83, 87–92, 155n28; of "obituary frame," 12, 108

Ghosts, 16–17, 22, 137–39, 141, 143. *See also* Figure

God: author as, 33–34, 40, 51; of machinery, 50–51

Goldmann, Lucien, 4

Grief, 11–12, 95–96, 100–101

Hegel, Georg Wilhelm Friedrich, 135, 140

Hospitality, 19; ethics of, 21, 25, 150n21

Huntington, Samuel, 125

Identity, 37, 117; writerly, 107–8. *See also* Queer theory

Immortality, 3, 34, 46–47

Infidelity/fidelity, 55–56, 77–82

Institution, 40; author as, 31, 37–38, 47–53

Iterability, 154n20

James, Henry, 88

Kant, Immanuel, 135, 140

Kofman, Sarah, 67, 153n13, 154n18

Law, 76–82

Lévinas, Emmanuel, 19–24, 61–62, 66, 147n22, 150n21

Lévi-Strauss, Claude, 4

Logic, 42; of the "and yet," 82; of ghosts, 137; perversity and, 7, 52, 82

Lorde, Audre, 17, 110, 141

Lynch, Michael, 12, 88, 99–109, 142, 158n27

Lyotard, Jean-François, 73–79, 97

Marx, Karl, 16–17, 135–41, 162n33

Mazhar, Farhad, 162n28

McLuhan, Marshall, 125

Memorial essay, 6–10, 20, 55, 58, 71–73, 82–83, 87–92, 155n28

Miller, D. A., 52

Moment, 30, 67, 70–71, 75–81; culture of the, 112–13; of death, 58; queer, 13, 89–92, 107–13; of

Moment (*continued*)
  reading, 7–9, 15, 56–57, 69. *See also* Temporality; Time
Moon, Michael, 101, 151n23, 151n26
Mourning: gaze of, 12, 108–9; politics of, 70; queer theory and, 88; theory and, 83; work and, 7, 10, 56, 64–66. *See also* Genre

Naas, Michael, 62–70, 75–81, 152n12, 153n16

Obituary: for Derrida, 23–24, 143; as frame, 12, 108; for Michael Lynch, 12, 99, 103–9, 158n27; queer temporality of, 105–6
Obsolescence, 15, 113, 117, 143
Other, the, 49–51, 67, 70, 77–82, 150n21, 155n25
Owens, Craig, 10–11, 13, 88, 92–102, 104, 105, 142

Parricide/deicide, 16, 137
"Part-objects," 92–93, 96, 100–102, 157n13
"Persistent present," 115–16, 121–25, 136
Perversity, 38–39; of the body, 40; of desire, 5, 11, 88, 93, 101; ethics and, 7; fantasy and, 44; logic and, 7, 52, 82; polymorphous, 149n13
Phonocentrism, 22, 25, 147n25
Pleasure, 44, 100, 102, 105, 158n25
Pleasure of the Text, The (Barthes),
  5, 30–31, 37–40, 49–50, 93–94, 150nn24–25
Poststructuralism, 1–2, 4, 29–31, 146n6
Print culture, temporality of, 13–14, 113–14, 121, 128
Proust, Marcel, 36–39, 47, 149n14

Queer theory, 5, 9, 11–12, 88, 90, 93, 101, 108
"Queer tutelage," 158n22
Quoting: ethics of, 70–71, 74, 76, 154n21; practice, 67, 74–80; violence of, 71–75, 78

Readers/reading, 7–8; of dead authors, 16–17, 20–22, 72–75, 87–88, 151n3; death of, 10; ethics of close reading and, 19–20, 24–25; mourning of, 6
Rembrandt van Rijn, 67, 154n18
Responsibility, 24, 63–64, 70–74, 77, 153n16
Riddel, Joseph, 68, 71, 75, 77
Rorty, Richard, 125
Rushdie, Salman, 2, 16

Sade, Fourier, Loyola (Barthes), 5–6, 9, 30–31, 35–49, 87–88
Saghafi, Kas, 63
Sarrasine (Balzac), 32, 33
Sedgwick, Eve Kosofsky, 18; Barthes and, 88, 92–93; *Between Men*, 94, 133; cancer of, 107–10; Derrida and, 87–88, 144; Lorde and, 17, 110, 141; Spivak and, 14, 15, 115–17, 124, 127–28, 141–44; "Tales of the Avunculate,"

100–101; *Tendencies*, 10–13, 17, 87–114

Sexuality: gay male, 52, 82; non-normative, 5; as perverse, 93, 101–2, 149n13; as queer, 93

Spivak, Gayatri Chakravorty, 18, 25; Barthes and, 16, 137–38, 162n30; *A Critique of Postcolonial Reason*, 14–17, 118–41; Derrida and, 159n7, 160n19, 161n23; Foucault and, 123, 129, 160n18, 160nn12–13; McLuhan and, 125; *In Other Worlds*, 118; *Outside in the Teaching Machine*, 118; Sedgwick and, 14, 15, 115–17, 124, 127–28, 141–44; "vanishing present" of, 14, 122–25, 127–30, 134, 142

Structuralism, 4, 146n6. *See also* Poststructuralism

Surprise, 99; from behind, 105, 158n25; death as, 105; fear and, 106; shock and, 104

Temporality, 8, 18, 25, 57, 71, 81–82, 97–99, 103, 118, 121, 158n29; of authorship, 15, 119, 124, 131; of books, 15; of ghosts, 137; indecent, 13; irony of, 104, 107; of progress, 130–36; queer, 9, 11–13, 88–89, 105, 113–16, 141; of writing, 13–14, 58, 110, 119, 142. *See also* Time

Tendencies (Sedgwick), 10–13, 17, 87–114

Theory, 143; as literary genre, 25; liveness and, 23–24, 26; mourning and, 83; of reading, 121–22; vanguardism of, 117

Thousand and One Nights, A, 3

Time, 8, 21, 25, 57, 81, 109, 118–19, 121, 123–24; lack of, 74, 154n21; as queer, 88–92; writing in, 9, 130, 136. *See also* Temporality

Trace, 41, 53, 147nn22–23; miracle of, 20–23, 25

Transmigration, 49–50

Transnational corporations, 123, 147n17

Transnational cultural studies, 128–30, 132, 134, 140

"Vanishing present" (Spivak), 14, 122–25, 127–30, 134, 142

Violence, 30, 32, 148n9, 155n22; complicity and, 16, 137; of interruption, 81; of quotation, 71–75, 78; of reading, 154n18

Voice, 20–26, 32–33, 79

"What Is an Author?" (Foucault), 2–4, 34, 42, 46

Work of Mourning, The (Derrida), 6–9, 64–65, 73–82, 97, 152n12

Yingling, Tom, 91, 92, 110

Jane Gallop is Distinguished Professor of English and

Comparative Literature at the University of Wisconsin,

Milwaukee. She is the author of several books, including

Living with His Camera (2003), *Anecdotal Theory* (2002),

Feminist Accused of Sexual Harassment (1997), *Around 1981:*

Academic Feminist Literary Theory (1992), and *Thinking*

through the Body (1988).

:: :: ::

Library of Congress Cataloging-in-Publication Data
Gallop, Jane, 1952–
The deaths of the author : reading and writing in time /
Jane Gallop.
p. cm.
Includes bibliographical references and index.
ISBN 978-0-8223-5063-7 (cloth : alk. paper)
ISBN 978-0-8223-5081-1 (pbk. : alk. paper)
1. Authorship—Psychological aspects. 2. Mortality.
3. Literary theory. 4. Queer theory. I. Title.
PN171.P83G355 2011
801′.95—dc22
2011006379